Zimbabwe:

Malaria Operational Plan FY 2014

TABLE OF CONTENTS

ACRONYMS AND ABBREVIATIONS

ACT	Artemisinin-based combination therapy
AL	Artemether/lumefantrine
ANC	Antenatal care
BCC	Behavior change communication
CDC	Centers for Disease Control and Prevention
CHW	Community health worker
DOT	Directly observed treatment
EHO	Environmental Health Officer
EHT	Environmental Health Technicians
FETP	Field epidemiology training program
FY	Fiscal year
GoZ	Government of Zimbabwe
HBMF	Home-based management of fever
HMIS	Health management information system
ICEMR	International Centers of Excellence for Malaria Research
IPTp	Intermittent preventive treatment of pregnant women
IPTp2	Intermittent preventive treatment for pregnant women with two or more doses
IRS	Indoor residual spraying
ITN	Insecticide-treated net
LLIN	Long-lasting insecticide-treated net
MCAZ	Medicine Control Authority of Zimbabwe
MCH	Maternal and child health
M&E	Monitoring and evaluation
MIP	Malaria in pregnancy
MoHCW	Ministry of Health and Child Welfare
NatPharm	National Pharmaceutical Company of Zimbabwe
NGO	Non-governmental organization
NIHR	National Institute of Health Research
NMCP	National Malaria Control Program
NMRL	National Microbiology Reference Laboratory
PERSUAP	Pesticide Evaluation Report and Safer Use Action Plan
PHCP	Primary health care package
PMI	President's Malaria Initiative
PPE	Personal protective equipment
QA/QC	Quality control/quality assurance
RBM	Roll Back Malaria
RDT	Rapid diagnostic test
SADC	Southern African Development Community
SARN	Southern Africa Regional Network
SP	Sulfadoxine-pyrimethamine

SSF	Single stream of funding (Global Fund Grant)
UNICEF	United Nations Children's Fund
USAID	United States Agency for International Development
USG	United States Government
VHW	Village health worker
WDSS	Weekly Disease Surveillance System
WHO	World Health Organization
WHT	Ward Health Team
ZINQAP	Zimbabwe National Quality Assurance Programme
ZIPS	Zimbabwe Informed Push System

EXECUTIVE SUMMARY

Malaria prevention and control are major foreign assistance objectives of the U.S. Government (USG). In May 2009, President Barack Obama announced the Global Health Initiative (GHI), a six year, comprehensive effort to reduce the burden of disease and promote healthy communities and families around the world. Through the GHI, the United States will help partner countries improve health outcomes, with a particular focus on improving the health of women, newborns, and children.

The President's Malaria Initiative (PMI) is a core component of the GHI, along with HIV/AIDS and tuberculosis programs. PMI was launched in June 2005 as a five year, $1.2 billion initiative to rapidly scale up malaria prevention and treatment interventions and reduce malaria-related mortality by 50% in 15 high-burden countries in sub-Saharan Africa by 2010. With passage of the 2008 Lantos-Hyde Act, funding for PMI was extended and, as part of the GHI, the goal of PMI was adjusted to reduce malaria-related mortality by 70% in the original 15 countries by the end of 2015.

In mid-2011, Zimbabwe's selection as a PMI country was announced. Malaria is a major health problem in Zimbabwe with 50% of the population at risk, although its epidemiology varies in the different regions of the country, ranging from year-round transmission in the lowland areas to epidemic-prone areas in the highlands. Zimbabwe's National Strategic Plan does not call for the implementation of all interventions in all malarious districts; hence the targeted number of districts varies by intervention, as detailed below.

Zimbabwe's malaria program receives support from two major donors, the Global Fund and PMI. United States Agency for International Development (USAID) provided targeted support to Zimbabwe's National Malaria Control Program (NMCP) through an emergency round of indoor residual spraying (IRS) in 2009 and in 2011 with a procurement of malaria commodities. Other malaria donors included UNICEF, the United Kingdom Department for International Development (DfID), and the European Commission. However, many European donors have shifted their funds to a new multi-donor fund designed to strengthen health systems in Zimbabwe, the Health Transition Fund. The Health Transition Fund is operating from 2011-2015 and aims to improve access to all types of quality health care for Zimbabweans and to harmonize donor support, practices, and requirements.

The FY 2014 Malaria Operational Plan was developed in collaboration with the NMCP and aligns well with the National Malaria Control Strategy. Planning for FY 2014 was carried out in Zimbabwe in April/May 2013 and included representatives from USAID and Centers for Disease Control and Prevention staff based in Washington, Atlanta, and Zimbabwe. The FY 2014 PMI proposed budget for Zimbabwe is $14 million. The following major activities will be supported with FY 2014 funding:

Insecticide-treated nets (ITNs): PMI is supporting the Ministry of Health and Child Welfare's (MoHCW) goal of universal coverage with 457,000 (FY 2011) and 700,000 (FY 2012) long-lasting insecticide-treated nets (LLINs) in 30 districts with moderate to high transmission of malaria. With FY 2013 funding, PMI will support planning for free routine distribution through antenatal care (ANC) and immunization clinics to pregnant women and children under one year of age through a pilot program to be implemented in 2013. With FY 2014 funding, PMI will procure approximately 525,000 LLINs for free routine distribution.

Indoor residual spraying (IRS): Zimbabwe has a long history of IRS dating back to the 1950s. The NMCP IRS strategy focuses on 45 high-burden malaria districts throughout the country. With FY 2012 funds focused on 17 districts, PMI supported spraying 581,165 structures, protecting approximately 1,164,586 persons. FY 2013 funding will support expansion from 17 to 22 districts, increasing the number of structures and population protected. With FY 2014 funding, PMI will support IRS operations in all pyrethroid spraying districts, spraying approximately 660,000 structures and protecting approximately 1.5 million people, primarily focusing on the three highly endemic provinces of Manicaland, Mashonaland East and Mashonaland West. Funding will cover the procurement of equipment for spray operations, training implementation, and environmental compliance for IRS in pyrethroid spraying areas. In addition, PMI will work with partners to support entomological monitoring and insecticide resistance.

Malaria in pregnancy (MIP): Zimbabwe's malaria in pregnancy policy focuses on the 30 high-burden malaria districts, and advocates for directly observed administration of three doses of sulfadoxine-pyrimethamine (SP). PMI supported the NMCP using FY 2012 funds to procure approximately 1 million treatments of SP, and plans to procure 500,000 treatments of SP with FY 2013 funding. With FY 2014 funding, PMI will support the NMCP by procuring approximately 285,000 treatments of SP. Funding will also be used to improve quantification of SP in an effort to minimize stock outs. In addition, PMI support will promote ITN use, early ANC visits and prompt malaria case management for pregnant women. Lastly, PMI and partners will work with NMCP to introduce the new WHO SP policy in Zimbabwe, which recommends giving IPTp at each antenatal care visit at least one month apart and starting after the second trimester.

Case management: Since 2007, the first-line treatment for malaria has been the artemisinin-based combination (ACT) drug, artemether-lumefantrine (AL). The NMCP policy requires that, where possible, all cases of malaria be diagnosed by microscopy or a rapid diagnostic test (RDT). At the end of 2010, the pharmacy board and the laboratory regulatory council changed the policy to allow community-based health workers to perform diagnosis using RDTs and dispense ACTs for positive cases. Historically, CHWs have included School Health Masters who taught malaria prevention and dispensed chloroquine but have not been a functional group for case management in the past five years, as well as village health workers (VHWs) who remain an active group. With FY 2014 funds, PMI will procure approximately 1.3 million ACTs and 3 million RDTs; strengthen the supply chain management system, known as the Zimbabwe Informed Push (ZIP) system; and support the training and promotion of quality service delivery by health facility and VHWs. The latter will include peer-to-peer supervision of VHWs.

Behavior change communication (BCC): Zimbabwe's 2008-2013 National Malaria Communication Strategy document utilizes advocacy, social mobilization, and BCC for malaria prevention and control through traditional and religious leaders and community volunteers organized into ward health teams (WHTs). The NMCP uses WHTs and community malaria committees to promote IRS campaigns and raise awareness about LLIN distribution and use. During the last quarter of 2013, PMI will support extension for the National Malaria

Communication Strategy from 2013 to 2015 in line with the National Malaria Control Strategy, as well as development of implementation guidelines for partners.

With FY 2014 funds, PMI will work with the NMCP and partners to strengthen BCC approaches for malaria prevention and treatment, particularly at the community level. PMI will be a major contributor to BCC activities supporting universal LLIN coverage, IRS, and IPTp, and will also collaborate in activities to improve malaria treatment-seeking and prevention behaviors.

Monitoring and evaluation (M&E): Prior to PMI support in Zimbabwe, the NMCP, with the support of Global Fund and other partners, developed a National Malaria M&E Strategy and Plan. The plan covers 2008-2013, and describes, by program area, the type of data needed, the indicators, data collection and flow, analysis, reporting, feedback and stakeholders' responsibilities.

With FY 2014 funding, PMI will strengthen M&E nationally by supporting training from the provincial level down to the primary health facility level. Training will be co-funded with Global Fund, and will include malaria stratification, improved reporting quality, epidemic surveillance and epidemic detection/response (through Integrated Disease Surveillance and Response curriculum). PMI will also contribute to the transition to DHIS2 through training/implementation workshops, focused on ways that benefit the malaria program directly.

PMI will support quarterly health facility surveys, through the end-use verification model, to assess the availability and appropriate use of malaria commodities. In addition, PMI funding will support anti-malarial drug efficacy studies of the front-line treatment, AL, in four of the country's eight sites.

PMI will support capacity building by contributing to the Field Epidemiology Training Program (FETP), a successful, twenty-year-old program in Zimbabwe, which is designed to train leaders in applied epidemiology while providing epidemiologic services to national and sub-national health care workers and supervisors.

Finally, PMI anticipates that a national level health survey will take place in 2015; it will be either a Malaria Indicator Survey or Demographic and Health Survey. PMI plans to support the planning and mobilization for the national level survey in consort with partners.

STRATEGY

1. Introduction

Global Health Initiative
Malaria prevention and control is a major foreign assistance objective of the U.S. Government (USG). In May 2009, President Barack Obama announced the Global Health Initiative (GHI) to reduce the burden of disease and promote healthy communities and families around the world. Through the GHI, the United States will help partner countries improve health outcomes, with a particular focus on improving the health of women, newborns and children. The GHI is a global commitment to invest in healthy and productive lives, building upon and expanding the USG's successes in addressing specific diseases and issues.

The GHI aims to maximize the impact the United States achieves for every health dollar it invests, in a sustainable way. The GHI's business model is based on: implementing a woman- and girl-centered approach; increasing impact and efficiency through strategic coordination and programmatic integration; strengthening and leveraging key partnerships, multilateral organizations, and private contributions; encouraging country ownership and investing in country-led plans and health systems; improving metrics, monitoring and evaluation; and promoting research and innovation. The GHI will build on the USG's accomplishments in global health, accelerating progress in health delivery and investing in a more lasting and shared approach through the strengthening of health systems.

President's Malaria Initiative
The President's Malaria Initiative (PMI) is a core component of the GHI, along with HIV/AIDS, and tuberculosis. PMI was launched in June 2005 as a 5-year, $1.2 billion initiative to rapidly scale up malaria prevention and treatment interventions and reduce malaria-related mortality by 50% in 15 high-burden countries in sub-Saharan Africa. With passage of the 2008 Lantos-Hyde Act, funding for PMI was extended and, as part of the GHI, the goal of PMI was adjusted to reduce malaria-related mortality by 70% in the original 15 countries by the end of 2015. This will be achieved by continuing to scale up coverage of the most vulnerable groups — children under five years of age (under five) and pregnant women — with proven preventive and therapeutic interventions, including artemisinin-based combination therapies (ACTs) for confirmed malaria cases, insecticide-treated nets (ITNs), intermittent preventive treatment of pregnant women (IPTp), and indoor residual spraying (IRS).

Zimbabwe was selected as a PMI country in FY 2011, but USAID has previously provided limited malaria support, including funding and technical assistance to conduct emergency IRS in 2009, and an emergency procurement of ACTs in early 2011. Funding for Zimbabwe has been:
- FY 2011, $12 million
- FY 2012, $14 million
- FY 2013, $15 million
- FY 2014, $14 million (planning figure)

This FY 2014 Malaria Operational Plan (MOP) presents a detailed implementation plan for Zimbabwe, based on the National Malaria Control Program's (NMCP's) extended National Malaria Control Strategy (2013-2015). PMI supported the extension of the Malaria Strategic Plan which was conducted through the participation of all stakeholders. The activities PMI is proposing to support align with the 2013-2015 National Malaria Control Strategy, and build upon investments made by other partners to improve and expand malaria-related services.

Zimbabwe's MOP FY 2014: 1) briefly reviews the current status of malaria control policies and interventions; 2) identifies challenges, opportunities and threats that pose barriers to achieving the targets of the NMCP and PMI; and 3) provides a description of planned FY 2014 activities.

2. Malaria Situation in Zimbabwe

Zimbabwe has seasonal and geographic variation in malaria transmission that corresponds closely with the country's rainfall pattern.

In general, the major malaria transmission season occurs during the rainy season between November and April, with the average temperature ranging between 18 and 30 degrees Celsius. The annual rainfall varies from less than 700 mm in the Matabeleland to more than 1,500 mm in Manicaland. Malaria transmission is lower in the low rainfall areas and higher in the high rainfall provinces.

Geographically, Zimbabwe is divided by a central watershed lying above 1,200 meters above sea level and flanked north and south by low lying areas. In 1986, the country was divided into three malaria epidemiological areas: areas below 900 meters to the north and below 600 meters in the south have perennial transmission; areas between 900-1,200 meters north and 600-900 meters south have seasonal transmission and are prone to epidemics; areas above 1,200 meters north and 900 meters in the south normally does not experience malaria transmission.[1]

---

[1] National Malaria Control Strategy 2008-2013, Ministry of Health and Child Welfare Zimbabwe.

Figure 2: Malaria transmission stratification, 2002

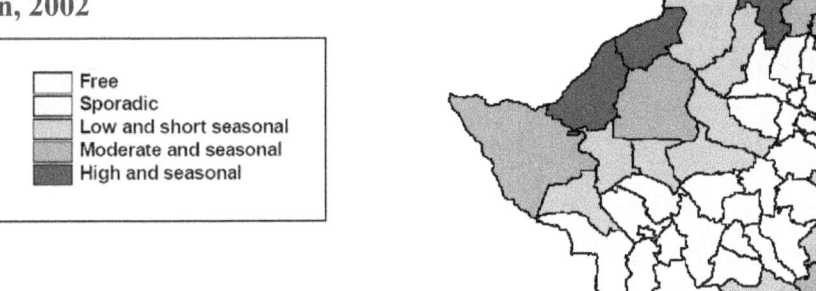

Free	
Sporadic	
Low and short seasonal	
Moderate and seasonal	
High and seasonal	

Zimbabwe is divided into ten provinces (two of which are considered urban), 62 rural districts and 1,200 wards. Forty-five of the rural districts are considered malarious, of those 30 are considered high malaria burden districts. Population estimates for Zimbabwe vary due to the recent migration within and outside the country. The present population estimate, according to the 2012 census, is 12.9 million. The 2002 malaria transmission stratification estimated that about half of the population lives in malaria risk areas. The map (Figure 3) below shows the burden of malaria by district for 2012.

Figure 3: Malaria incidence rates per 1,000 population by district, 2012

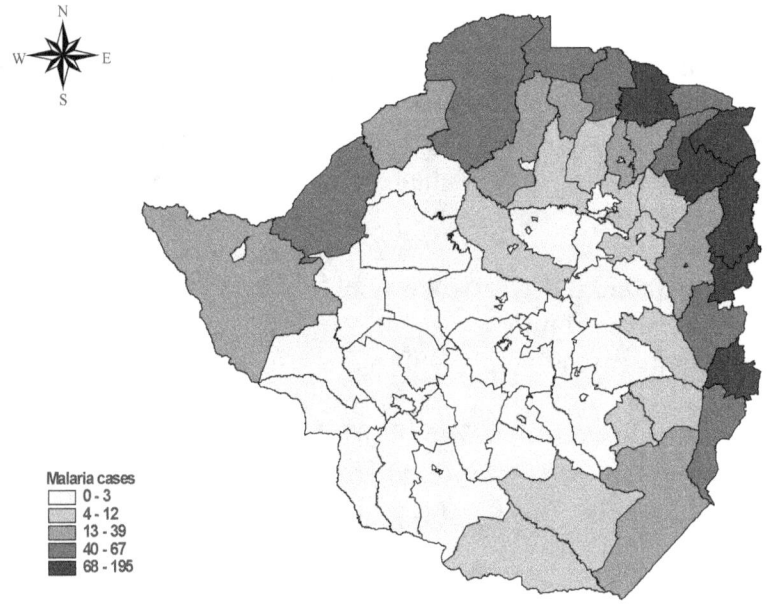

Malaria cases
0 - 3	
4 - 12	
13 - 39	
40 - 67	
68 - 195	

Malaria burden
Overall, malaria incidence in Zimbabwe appears to be decreasing even though it remains a major challenge in certain districts and wards. According to the NMCP latest figures, malaria incidence

decreased from 1.8 million cases in 2006 to 331,772 cases in 2012.[2] Outpatient department malaria cases have decreased from about 1.53 million in 2005 to approximately 659,262 in 2011; inpatient malaria cases declined from 53,000 in 2005 to 26,000 in 2011 with case fatality rate for same period oscillating from 4.02% in 2005 to 5.6% in 2007 to 4.51% (per 100,000) in 2011. By December 2010, Zimbabwe's reported malaria incidence rate was 49 cases per 1,000, indicating a decline of almost 64% from the 2000 data. It is difficult to know how much of the reduction is due to migration, drought, a weakened surveillance system, or if this represents a true reduction due to effective malaria control interventions.

Figure 4: Trends of malaria incidence per 1,000 population, 2000-2012

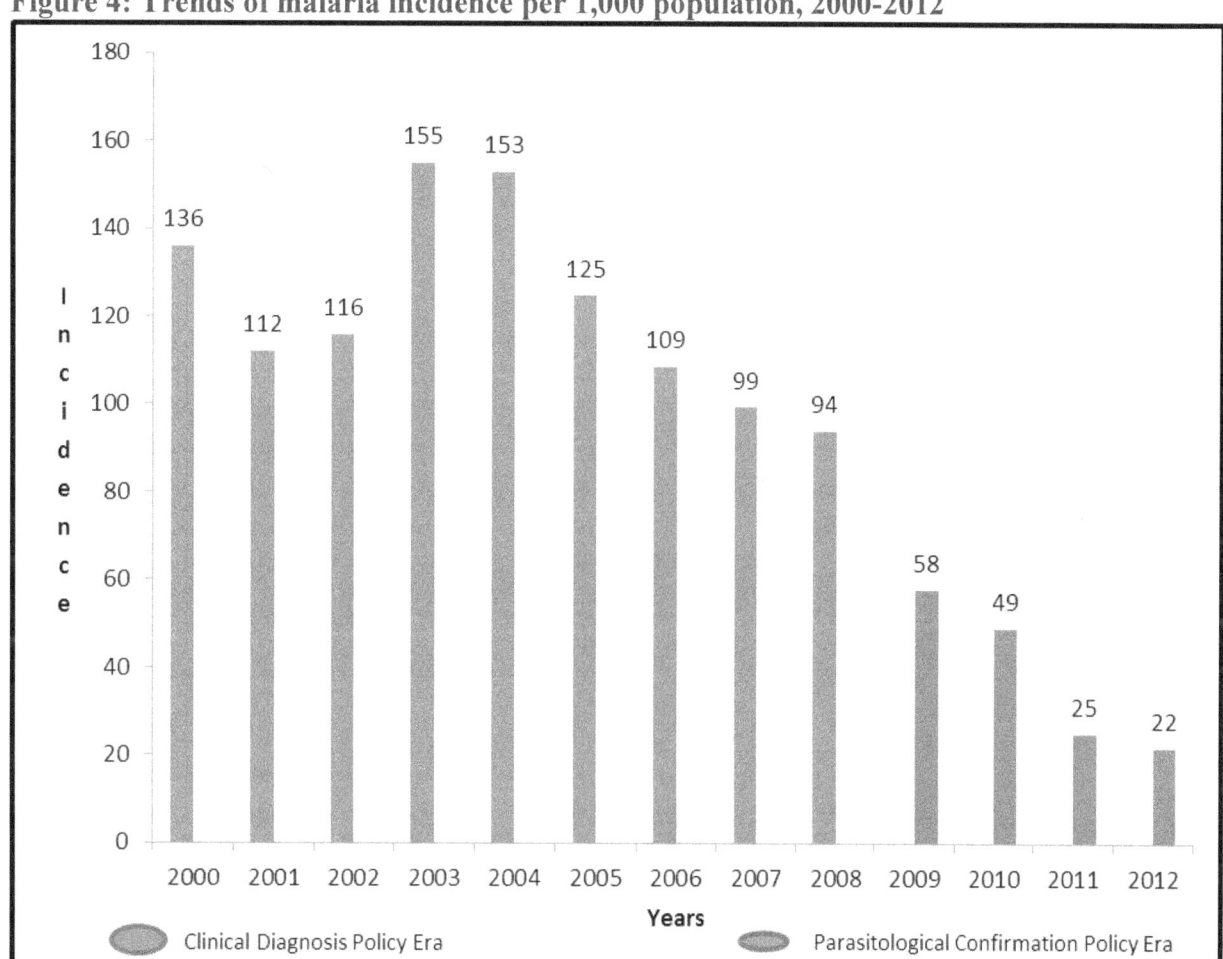

Note: The 2001 drop in cases was attributed to health workers "industrial action" that paralyzed the health system. Since 2008 there have been no inpatient morbidity and mortality data at national level due to problems of computer software changes.

Plasmodium falciparum accounts for 98% of all reported malaria cases; *P. ovale* and *P. malariae* account for the remaining 2%. The CDC light traps and pyrethrum spray catches conducted at

---

2 Zimbabwe Malaria Program Review (draft), Ministry of Health and Child Welfare (2012)

PMI supported sentinel sights in 2013 showed the major malaria vector to be *An. gambiae s.l*, with other vectors such as *An. pretoriensis, An. funestus* and *An. rufipes* also present (Source: AIRS Project). *An. quadriannulatus,* a member of the *An. gambiae complex*, is commonly found in Zimbabwe, but is zoophilic and therefore not a malaria vector. A fourth member of the complex, *An. Merus,* which is a vector in coastal areas of Eastern Africa, has also been reported in Zimbabwe; its role in malaria transmission is unclear.

3. National Malaria Control Program: Plan and Strategy

The MoHCW has three main divisions: Policy Planning, Monitoring and Evaluation; Curative Services; and Preventive Services, plus the Provincial Medical Directorates. Under the Preventive Services directorate is the Epidemiology and Disease Control Department and the NMCP is located within this department. The NMCP is led by a program manager, supported by a team of senior officers responsible for: case management, monitoring and evaluation (M&E), vector control, behavioral change communication (BCC), and finance and administration.

At the provincial level, the Provincial Medical Director is responsible for all health activities, including malaria control, and has a team of managers responsible for Epidemiology and Disease Control, nursing services, environmental health, administration, nutrition, health promotion and pharmacy. The Epidemiology and Disease Control manager also serves as the provincial focal person for malaria. The structure at the district level mirrors the province with a District Health Executive. The district health team is led by the District Medical Officer, who is responsible for malaria activities, among others, and works with ward health teams (WHTs) to coordinate and implement health programs. The Environmental Health Officer (EHO) manages IRS activities; the district nursing officer is responsible for case management training.

The primary health facility level is staffed by two nurses, Environmental Health Technicians (EHTs) and nurse aides. There are approximately 1,500 primary health facilities in Zimbabwe and each primary health facility is linked to a WHT comprised of community members such as village health workers, school health teachers, headmen, chiefs, and religious leaders. The health facility staff is responsible for overseeing program implementation in conjunction with the WHT. The WHT members are volunteers, although trained community-based health volunteers receive incentive of $14/month from the Global Fund single stream grant for health system strengthening.

The NMCP collaborates with diverse partners and has linkages with the following parastatal organizations:
- National Pharmaceutical Company of Zimbabwe (NatPharm), which is responsible for the procurement, storage and distribution of all health commodities, including malaria commodities;
- Medicine Control Authority of Zimbabwe (MCAZ), which is responsible for registration of all medicines in the country;
- National Microbiology Reference Laboratory (NMRL), which is responsible for internal quality assurance; and

- Zimbabwe National Quality Assurance Programme (ZINQAP), which is responsible for external quality assurance for laboratories.

The NMCP has 11 members of national level staff and 8 provincial malaria focal persons; all currently supported by the Global Fund malaria grant. At the national level, the NMCP develops policy, national guidelines and training materials. The national level also oversees program implementation, monitoring and evaluation, resources mobilization and coordinates partnerships. Due to Zimbabwe's economic collapse in 2008/2009, all of the NMCP positions in Harare are supported by the Global Fund. The position of the Provincial Malaria Focal Person is also supported by the Global Fund while the other workers receive allowances from the Zimbabwe Health Worker Retention Scheme.

The Government of Zimbabwe (GoZ) and partners fund the malaria program. The budget is planned annually, based upon district annual plans which are consolidated at the provincial and later the national levels.

Table 1: Malaria funding 2008-2014

Partners	2008	2009	2010	2011	2012	2013	2014
GoZ	$850,000	$1,400,000	$1,200,000	$1,000,000	902,850	1,200,000	*
Global Fund	2,100,000	11,320,000	24,500,000	2,600,000	19,069,239	7,460,006	8,348,313
WHO (CERF)		-	1,200,000	79,000	-	150,000	
UNICEF	320,000	450,000	25,000	18,250	42,500		
PMI	-	200,000	1,000,000	12,000,000	14,000,000	14,000,000	14,000,000
DFID	-	300,000	-	-			
Private Sector	47,250	60,000	20,000	12,500			
Total	**$3,317,250**	**$14,930,000**	**$25,745,000**	**$15,612,500**	**33,069,239**	**21,460,006**	**22,348,313**

Note: the GoZ line items reflect activities funded in foreign currency only. This figure does not include human resource and infrastructure maintenance related costs which currently is covered by Global Fund.
* Data forthcoming

In addition to the above financial assistance, the European Commission, along with other local and international non-governmental organizations (NGOs), supports malaria control activities.

The NMCP's 2003-2015 extended National Strategic Plan was updated in 2013. The vision of the plan is a malaria-free Zimbabwe, and the goal is to "reduce malaria incidence from 95/1,000 in 2007 to 10/1,000 by 2015 and reduce malaria deaths to near zero by 2015." The five key approaches to the National Strategy include:
- Universal access to malaria prevention and personal protection with: 90% of the population at risk covered by IRS and ITNs, and 85% coverage of two or more recommended doses of intermittent preventive treatment for pregnant women (IPTp2) attending antenatal care in medium-high transmission areas.
- Improve diagnosis and treatment of both uncomplicated and severe malaria.

- Improve detection and timely control of malaria epidemics, by detecting at least 95% of malaria epidemics within two weeks of onset.
- Strengthen community and other stakeholder participation to maximize achievement of universal access to malaria control interventions.
- Improve partnership coordination, financial and human resources management and malaria surveillance monitoring.

The Zimbabwe NMCP participates in a number of sub-regional and cross-border initiatives. The program is an active partner with the Roll Back Malaria (RBM) Southern Africa Regional Network (SARN) and with the Southern African Development Community (SADC) malaria network. NMCP is a member of the Malaria Elimination (E8) countries. The program is also a member of the Trans-Zambezi Malaria Initiative with Zimbabwe, Zambia, Namibia and Botswana, and MOZIZA, the cross-border malaria initiative with Mozambique, Zimbabwe and South Africa.

4. Goals and Targets of the President's Malaria Initiative

The goal of PMI is to reduce malaria-associated mortality by 50% compared to pre-initiative levels in the 15 original PMI countries. By the end of 2015, PMI will assist Zimbabwe to achieve the following targets in populations at risk for malaria:

- >90% of households with a pregnant woman and/or children under five will own at least one ITN
- 85% of children under five will have slept under an ITN the previous night
- 85% of pregnant women will have slept under an ITN the previous night
- 85% of houses in geographic areas targeted for IRS will have been sprayed
- 85% of pregnant women and children under five will have slept under an ITN the previous night or in a house that has been sprayed with IRS in the last 6 months
- 85% of women who have completed a pregnancy in the last two years will have received two or more doses of IPTp during that pregnancy
- 85% of government health facilities have ACTs available for treatment of uncomplicated malaria
- 85% of children under five with suspected malaria will have received treatment with ACTs within 24 hours of onset of their symptoms.

5. Current Status of Malaria Indicators

As in many African countries, PMI and the NMCP rely on nationally representative health surveys to track progress in coverage of malaria control interventions in Zimbabwe. There have been five such surveys since 2005. The most recent three surveys have been a Multiple Indicator Monitoring Survey (MIMS) conducted by UNICEF from August to October 2009, the Demographic Health Survey (DHS) carried out from September 2010 to March 2011, and a Malaria Indicator Survey (MIS) conducted in February to April of 2012. The latter was conducted by NMCP with support from the Global Fund and PMI. Data from the 2012 MIS will provide baseline for key PMI indicators. The next DHS is planned for 2015/16.

Zimbabwe has achieved steady gains in many key malaria indicators. Between the 2005 and 2012 ITN ownership and use and the uptake of IPTp2 have increased significantly (Table 2). These data are encouraging but also suggest that efforts to scale up interventions must continue for Zimbabwe to achieve the RBM, PMI, and national targets.

The 2010 DHS shows national ITN ownership of one or more ITNs averaged 29% for the country compared to 9% in 2005, and the 2012 MIS found a higher proportion of ITN ownership (46%) in the 51 malaria endemic districts that were sampled. The 2010 DHS found that 10% of children under five reported sleeping under an ITN the previous night compared to 50% in the 51 malaria endemic districts sampled in the 2012 MIS.

Table 2. Estimates of Malaria Indicators, 2005-2012

Indicator	2005 DHS	2009 MIMS	2010 DHS	2012 MIS*
Proportion of households with one or more ITNs	9%	27%	29%	46%
Proportion of children under five years old who slept under an ITN the previous night	4%	17%	10%	57.9%
Proportion of pregnant women who slept under an ITN the previous night	NA	NA	10%	NA**
Proportion of women of child-bearing age who slept under an ITN the previous night	NA	NA	NA	44.6%
Proportion of women who received two or more doses of IPTp during their last pregnancy in the last two years	NA	NA	7%	35%
Proportion of children under five years old with fever in the last two weeks who received treatment with ACTs	5%	14%	2%	NA

*MIS was conducted in 51 malaria endemic districts of eight rural provinces
**Data was collected on net use by women of child bearing age but not among pregnant women specifically

6. Integration, Collaboration, Coordination

Both USAID and CDC support programs in three key areas of GHI: HIV/AIDS, tuberculosis (TB) and malaria. With FY 2014 funding, PMI/Zimbabwe will actively seek opportunities to collaborate with other USG health programs so as to ensure maximum impact for every health dollar the United States Government invests in the country. Opportunities include the following:

Maternal and child health services and malaria: Since malaria prevention and control activities have been implemented as part of integrated maternal and child health services, PMI will make a significant contribution to strengthening capacity to deliver these services. PMI/Zimbabwe will work with other USG-funded programs and other partners to support the comprehensive primary health care package, including the training and implementation of community-based diagnosis and treatment of fever, IPTp, and early treatment. PMI will continue to support universal coverage of LLINs via campaigns as well as the integration of LLIN distribution within routine ANC and EPI services. PMI will also support the strengthening of supply chains, including support for the Zimbabwe Informed Push System (ZIPS), which includes tuberculosis commodities, primary health care packages, and malaria commodities, namely rapid diagnostic tests (RDTs), sulfadoxine-pyrimethamine (SP), and ACTs.

HIV/AIDS and malaria: The seroprevalence of HIV infections is high at an estimated 15.2% among individuals aged 15 to 49 years old.[3] Infection with HIV is higher among women (17.7%) than men (12.3%) and is higher in urban areas (7.0%) than in rural (4.8%) areas.

Areas where integration will be pursued between the HIV/AIDS Program and NMCP include: promoting adherence to universal precautions when taking blood samples, integrating laboratory quality assurance, providing LLINs to people living with HIV/AIDS, and ensuring appropriate malaria prevention services at Prevention of Mother-to-Child Transmission clinics. At the community level, PMI will support VHWs who provide RDT and ACT services to also communicate important messages regarding HIV prevention and testing.

Tuberculosis and Malaria: The National Tuberculosis Program supports the activities of village health promoters to inform and support TB diagnosis and follow-up. Where these promoters are the same as the VHWs that provide RDT/ACT services, PMI will work to integrate activities across HIV, tuberculosis, and malaria.

Commitment to reducing the malaria burden and continuing on the path of malaria elimination is evident at the highest levels of the MoHCW. The NMCP staff meet weekly to review work plans and monitor progress. The NMCP coordinates with partners through five malaria technical subcommittees: vector control, M&E, case management, BCC, and procurement and supply management. These sub-committees are chaired by the NMCP staff, include all PMI Implementing Partners as appropriate, and meet quarterly.

The NMCP participates actively in the "Health Cluster" group meetings, chaired by the WHO. Also, the Health Partners Development Group meets on a quarterly basis to discuss issues of mutual interest. Currently the European Union chairs these meetings.

PMI, led by the PMI in-country team, will work closely with the NMCP, RBM partners, Global Fund-funded and other health-related programs in Zimbabwe to provide integrated services at the health facility and community level. PMI will work with others in USAID/Zimbabwe to ensure coordination of PMI-supported activities within the broader context of the health strategies. These approaches will ensure the most cost-effective implementation of prevention and

---

[3] Zimbabwe 2010/11 Demographic Health Survey

treatment measures. PMI and NMCP have agreed on a quarterly PMI implementing partners meeting, which includes PMI Resident Advisors, partners, and the NMCP.

In addition, PMI staff will provide leadership and technical assistance in other coordinating bodies such as the local RBM (including relevant RBM sub-committees). At the planning and implementation levels, PMI and other partners will work together to effectively fill commodity and human resource gaps.

8. PMI Support Strategy and Expected Results

PMI works through partners that operate under the leadership of NMCP. Through this strategy PMI works to complement and fill in gaps that remain a challenge from Global Fund and GoZ funding.

FY 2014 Expected Results – Prevention
1. PMI will procure and distribute approximately 525,000 free LLINs in the 30 districts targeted for universal coverage in Zimbabwe.

2. PMI will continue to support universal IRS in all the pyrethroid districts, covering approximately 660,000 structures, protecting approximately 1.5 million people in the targeted IRS districts.

FY 2014 Expected Results – Treatment
1. PMI will procure approximately 1.3 million ACT treatments for uncomplicated malaria and distribute them to primary health facilities and village health workers throughout the country.

2. PMI will procure approximately 3 million RDTs for distribution to primary health facilities and village health workers.

9. Challenges, Opportunities, and Threats

The current USG restrictions prohibiting funding directly to the GoZ or any institution affiliated with the GoZ, make it challenging to implement NMCP-led activities in Zimbabwe. However, both major malaria donors (PMI and Global Fund) work through partners that operate under the leadership of NMCP; planning and working closely with NMCP staff throughout all activities. District health staff, including EHTs, and health facility workers are responsible for malaria prevention and control activities implementation in communities, including the training and supervision of VHWs. Because of current USG policy in Zimbabwe, PMI is unable to support government staff per diem or allowances for routine monitoring visits to the field which are critical for a successful program implementation; and there are seldom funds available for supervision from GoZ. Therefore, ensuring that monitoring visits occur and that staff are compensated is a particular challenge.

OPERATIONAL PLAN

1. Insecticide-Treated Nets

NMCP/PMI Objectives

Zimbabwe's National Malaria Strategic Plan calls for universal coverage with LLINs in moderate to high transmission areas which includes 30 of the country's 62 districts (Figure 5). However, the NMCP is considering expansion of LLIN coverage areas more broadly throughout the country in the near future, even perhaps including coverage of the entire country. The motivation for the expansion is unclear and currently under discussion among NMCP and partners.

The NMCP definition for universal coverage is evolving. It began as one net for every two persons, expanded to include at least one net per sleeping place, which is estimated at least three nets per household. The NMCP intends to: 1) increase the proportion of the general population sleeping under an LLIN to 80%, 2) increase household ownership of at least three LLINs to 100%, and 3) increase the number of children under five and pregnant women sleeping under an LLIN to 85% by 2015. The NMCP supports a mixed model of ITN distribution that includes distribution through public health facilities, community-based fixed-point campaigns, and mop-up, door-to-door campaigns. However, currently the NMCP relies solely on distribution through mass campaigns (fixed point distribution followed by mop-up, door-to-door distribution). A system for routine distribution of LLINs through public health facilities has not yet been developed; but is part of the National Strategy and planned to be developed by the end of 2013.

Figure 5: Targeted LLIN and IPTp Districts in Zimbabwe, 2013

From 2008 to 2010, a total of 1.9 million LLINs were distributed free to targeted communities. Global Fund Round 8 phase 1 procured 1,219,309 LLINs and UNITAID procured 640,557 LLINs in 2009. The LLINs distributed by 2010 are estimated to have covered 83% of the population in the 30 targeted districts, assuming that one LLIN is shared between two people. The majority of these LLINs were distributed through mass campaigns using public health facilities as fixed distribution points. Before each distribution cycle, a census was carried out to determine the number of individuals in the home and estimate nets required.

According to the 2010-2011 DHS, 29% of households owned at least one ITN and 10% of children under five and 10% of pregnant women slept under an ITN the previous night.

Data from the 2012 MIS, in the 30 LLIN target districts, found that:
- 55.7% of households had at least one net
- 19.8% of households had more than one net

Among households that had a net (any variety net), 83.3% had at least one LLIN and 32.2% had more than one LLIN.

Global Fund (Rounds 8 and 10) has been the primary development partner providing technical assistance for ITN procurement and distribution. The following table outlines the LLINs already procured and expected to be procured in the coming years:

Table 3: LLINs delivered and pledged by donor

Donor	2012 (procured)	2013 (procured)	2014 (pledged)	2015 (pledged)
Global Fund	2,000,000	1,300,000	Unknown	unknown
PMI	457,000	700,000	1,400,000	525,000
UMCOR	45,437	0	Unknown	Unknown
Total	2,502,437	2,000,000	1,400,000	525,000

Universal coverage in Zimbabwe was expected to be achieved by 2013; but with the revised goal of a malaria-free Zimbabwe by 2015, the ITN specific objectives have been/are being updated. In calculating a net gap for Zimbabwe, the information above, estimated population growth, and number of nets per person were considered.

Table 4: LLIN needs/gap based on persons protected

Criteria if using nets per person	Country data
At-risk population 2013	9,368,934
Expected annual population growth	3%
Average number of persons per net	2(/1.8)
Distributed LLINs	
Distributed LLINs in 2010	1,219,309
Distributed LLINs in 2011	N/A
Distributed LLINs in 2012	2,502,437
Distributed LLINs in 2013	2,000,000
Pledged LLINs	
Pledged LLINs for distribution in 2014	1,400,000
Pledged LLINs for distribution in 2015	525,000

Calculations for 2015

Population at risk in 2015	9,472,001
Total number of LLINs needed (/1.8)	5,262,222
Number of existing nets	4,138,000
Nets distributed plus pledged	1,400,000
Estimated Actual Gap	599,222

Progress during the past 12 months

With FY 2012 funds, PMI procured 700,000 LLINs. These LLINs will be used to meet the universal coverage targets through campaigns in targeted districts in July 2013. Logistics planning for the campaign has begun and will follow on the recent 2013 Global Fund LLIN distribution; but exact districts and distribution points are not yet selected. PMI/Global Fund partners prepared a community mobilization plan and printed materials for the campaign. Door-to-door household audits will be used to create a net roster; and an LLIN card designated for each household.

Planning for routine LLIN distribution using antenatal and child health clinics will begin in late 2013 at the national and provincial level with expertise from a project with worldwide experience in planning for routine distribution. The specific channel(s) for distribution will be identified during this planning process.

Plans and justification

The NMCP is planning to continue LLIN campaign waves through 2014 in the targeted 30 LLIN districts. The Global Fund Single Stream of Funding (SSF) grant, combining Rounds 8 and 10 is supporting the procurement of 1.3 million LLINs in 2013. The NMCP expects that a new Global Fund grant opportunity will occur around September or October 2013. A proposal from NMCP will include LLIN procurement and distribution as is reflected in a gap analysis already produced in anticipation of the grant. The PMI FY 2013 and FY 2014 funding is providing support to procure an additional 950,000 and 525,000 LLINs, respectively, primarily to support the campaign waves through 2014 with the remaining LLINs for routine distribution to pregnant women via ANC and families via child health clinics or schools.

Challenges, opportunities, and threats

The current USG restrictions prohibiting funding directly to the GoZ or any institution affiliated with the GoZ, make it challenging to implement NMCP-led LLIN activities in Zimbabwe. However, both major malaria donors (PMI and Global Fund) work through partners that operate under the leadership of NMCP, planning and working closely with NMCP staff throughout all activities. The Global Fund operates LLIN campaigns via one of the same PMI implementing partners which allows for advantageous synergies.

District health staff, including, EHTs, and health facility workers are responsible for LLIN implementation in communities, including the training and supervision of VHWs. Because of current USG policy in Zimbabwe, PMI is unable to support government staff per diem or allowances for routine monitoring visits to the field; and there are seldom funds available for supervision from GoZ. Therefore, ensuring that monitoring visits occur and that staff are compensated is a particular challenge.

Proposed activities with FY 2014 funding ($2,450,000)

Following discussions with the NMCP, PMI will continue to fill gaps in ITN procurement not covered by the Global Fund and the GoZ. Using FY 2014 funding, PMI support will target LLIN procurement and distribution for a new continuous distribution approach designed to ensure high ITN coverage of new cohorts of pregnant women and children, and to replace worn out LLINs distributed through the campaigns.

Specific activities to be supported by PMI in FY2014 include:

1. *Procure LLINs for routine replacement and keep-up distribution:* Procure approximately 525,000 LLINs for distribution primarily through campaigns and a small amount to be determined through routine distribution, through channels identified during planning, such as routine antenatal clinic (ANC), child health clinics, and schools to maintain coverage of vulnerable populations. Geographic targeting will depend on previous campaign results, the status of improvements to routine distribution systems rollout, and MOH guidance. *($2,000,000)*

2. *Planning, distribution, and monitoring of routine LLIN distribution systems:* PMI will provide support to the NMCP in logistics and operations to strengthen continuous LLIN distribution systems and supply chain management to promote continuous availability of

LLINs to people who need them and to strengthen the distribution systems capacity for efficient delivery of LLINs to end users. *($450,000)*

3. *Technical assistance to implement LLIN activities*: One USAID technical assistance visit to support overall LLIN distributions. *(amount included in core PMI budget)*

2. Indoor Residual Spraying

NMCP/PMI Objectives

Zimbabwe has a long history of implementing IRS, dating back to 1949. Currently, the NMCP IRS strategy targets one round of spraying in the 45 malarious districts. There is not yet an articulated strategy on the combination or balance of IRS and LLINs, and LLINs continue to be distributed in the 30 districts with the highest malaria burden. According to the 2010-2011 DHS, 17% of households received IRS within the past 12 months. This figure ranged from 40% in higher-burden malaria provinces (Matabeleland North) to 2% in Harare, where there is little or no malaria transmission. The 2012 MIS showed that 48.6% of households in the 45 targeted districts were sprayed within the past 12 months. This figure ranged from 65.6% in Mashonaland East to 36.3% in Mashonaland West.

The program used DDT until 1991, when it was replaced with pyrethroids. However, after the switch, a marked increase in reported malaria cases was observed, prompting the reintroduction of DDT in 2004. The IRS program continues with a mix of DDT and pyrethroids, where DDT is used only in non-commercial agricultural areas. In 2013, the NMCP plans to spray 22 districts with DDT, and the remaining 23 districts with pyrethroids.

Due to financial constraints, the total number of rooms sprayed and population protected from 2001-2007 were below the targets as shown in the table below. From 2008 to 2010, funding from the Global Fund, the European Commission, DfID and USAID increased and IRS coverage expanded.

Table 5: Rooms* sprayed and population covered 2001-2012

Season	Target Rooms	Rooms sprayed	% Coverage	Target Pop	Pop protected	% Pop. Protected
2001	1,191,950	762,848	64	1,602,334	1,229,798	77
2002	2,235,151	680,577	30	4,732,872	1,022,603	44
2003	2,235,151	284,128	28	4,732,872	435,748	20
2004	2,175,026	1,350,403	62	3,373,034	2,031,509	60
2005	1,839,727	1,271,474	69	1,875,472	1,608,848	86
2006	1,764,368	1,212,572	69	2,920,561	1,659,393	57
2007	1,413,074	588,994	42	2,436,172	742,289	30
2008	1,111,663	958,045	85	1,630,915	1,242,346	80
2009	1,992,181	1,638,303	86	3,096,049	2,575,116	86
2010	2,255,318	2,023,159	90	3,478,413	3,090,289	89
2011	2,423,091	2,150,383	93	3,496,756	3,299,058	92
2012	2,420,141	2,159,297	90	3,540,128	3,106,659	87

* Zimbabwe's IRS data is recorded as rooms sprayed. PMI's IRS implementing partner has developed an algorithm to equate rooms sprayed to structures sprayed, based on the 2012 IRS campaign, which is found later in this section.

Indoor residual spraying training occurs at three levels: for provincial managers, for IRS district managers, and for spray operators. The Zimbabwe NMCP uses a variety of training materials developed by the program itself, by WHO, and by the major insecticide manufacturers. In addition to hands-on spraying practice, training includes presentations on malaria epidemiology and entomology. Health and safety issues are also included in the IRS training, including the provision and use of personal protective equipment (PPE) and safe handling of pesticides.

Technical support and coordination for entomological monitoring in Zimbabwe is provided by the National Institute of Health Research (NIHR), formerly known as the "Blair Institute." During the early 1990s, vector mapping and vector bionomics were identified as priority activities along with insecticide susceptibility monitoring and bioassay assessments. A total of 16 entomological monitoring sites, two sites per province, were established with Global Fund support. While these sites do have some equipment and some staff have been trained, support is needed to ensure consistent entomological surveillance across all sites.

Where PMI is supporting IRS, there are some data that the vectors remain susceptible to the insecticides that are being applied, as the following tables indicate. Wall bioassays are routinely done after spraying, using locally collected *An. gambae*.

Table 6: Mortality rates of *Anopheles gambiae s.l* field populations from Kawere (Mutoko District, Mashonaland East Province), March 2013

Insecticide	Kawere			
	Total tested (replicates)	KD* after 30 min (%)	KD after 60 min (%)	% mortality 24-hour
Lambda-cyhalothrin (0.05%)	35 (2)	17.14%	91.43%	90.83%
Deltamethrin (0.05%)	30 (2)	36.67%	100%	100%
Bendiocarb (0.1%)	30 (2)	63.33%	100%	100%
DDT (4%)	18 (1)	61.11%	100%	100%
Pirimiphos-methyl (1.0%)	15 (1)	0%	80%	100%
Silicone Oil (Pyrethroid control)	20 (1)	0%	0%	0%
Olive Oil (OP/carbamate control)	15 (1)	0%	0%	0%
Risella Oil (OC control)	15 (1)	0%	0%	0%

*KD = knockdown
Source: AIRS Project –March 2013

Table 7: Mortality rates of *Anopheles gambiae s.l* field populations from Kasimure (Hurungwe District, Mashonaland West Province), March 2013

Insecticide	Kasimure			
	Total tested (replicates)	KD after 30 min (%)	KD after 60 min (%)	% mortality 24-hour
Lambda-cyhalothrin (0.05%)	31 (2)	12.9%	67.74%	90%
Deltamethrin (0.05%)	29 (2)	93.10%	93.10%	93.75%
Bendiocarb (0.1%)	42 (2)	88.09%	88.09%	100%
DDT (4%)	24 (1)	95.83%	95.83%	100%
Pirimiphos-methyl (1.0%)	21 (1)	85.71%	85.71%	100%
Silicone Oil (Pyrethroid control)	15 (1)	0%	0%	0%
Olive Oil (OP/carbamate control)	15 (1)	0%	0%	0%
Risella Oil (OC control)	15 (1)	0%	0%	0%

Source: AIRS Project – March 2013

At the national level, the Vector Control Subcommittee, including partners and vector control experts, meets quarterly or more frequently during the spray season to provide guidance and technical advice to the NMCP. An M&E framework tracks inputs, outputs, and outcomes of the spraying, as well as entomological monitoring. Standard indicators include the proportion of the targeted rooms sprayed, the proportion of the targeted population protected, refusal rates, amounts of insecticide consumed, and average daily spray rates. Although the NCMP monitors IRS by using 'rooms sprayed,' for the purposes of PMI reporting, 'structures sprayed' will be tracked.

Progress during the past 12 months

PMI began support for IRS activities in Zimbabwe in 2012 by conducting a Supplemental Environmental Assessment (SEA) to the Programmatic Environmental Assessment, to ensure that IRS activities will not adversely impact the environment, people, or bio-diversity in the country.

In 2012/13, PMI supported spraying in 17 districts in three high burden provinces: Mashonaland East, Mashonaland West, and Manicaland. A total of 501,613 structures were sprayed, achieving 86% coverage and protecting 1,164,586 people. With PMI support, 968 spray operators and support staff were trained in spray operations and environmental compliance, plus 37 health workers were trained in IRS solid waste management. PMI supported the construction of 65 soak pits for proper disposal of liquid pyrethroid waste. PMI funding also procured 899 sets of PPE to support 36 spray teams.

Routine entomological monitoring has been conducted with PMI funding in five sentinel sites. Insecticide susceptibility tests on all four classes of insecticide were conducted (see tables above), and cone bio-assays to verify the quality of spraying was carried out in four sites. The quality data for Murara site are presented in the figure below.

Figure 6: Mortality rates of field–collected *Anopheles gambiae s.l.* after exposure to insecticide sprayed surfaces at Murara sentinel site (Mashonaland East Province). Lambda-cyhalothrin (10WP) was sprayed in Murara.

In addition, PMI funding supported entomological data collection on indoor resting and vector densities. Pyrethrum spray collections were conducted in Murara, Kasimure, Burma Valley, Kawere, and the control sites of Rusike and Strathlone Farm. The CDC light traps were used and showed that mosquito densities varied among the six above-mentioned sites. This is not uncommon.

Plans and justification

Due to the NMCP's experience and capabilities to conduct IRS, PMI support will not encompass the entire IRS package, as in other countries. Instead, PMI will work with the NMCP to fill IRS operational gaps and establish a robust insecticide resistance management system.

PMI will focus IRS support to all pyrethroid districts, increasing from 17 districts to 22, while also providing technical support to nationwide activities, including environmental compliance, IEC messaging for IRS, and strengthening of the data collection and M&E system. On-going entomological surveillance will be conducted in a portion of the 16 established sentinel sites, including additional studies as to the potential emerging pyrethoid resistance. Once PMI's implementing partner completes the sentinel site assessment, slated for late 2013, then PMI will determine how many sites to support.

Challenges, opportunities, and threats

The EHTs and health facility workers are responsible for IRS implementation in the communities, including the training of trainers, and IRS supervision. Since PMI is unable to support staff per diems or allowances for monitoring visits to the field, ensuring that monitoring visits occur and that staff are compensated is a challenge. The same difficulties are applicable to the research officers under the NIHR, who would normally lead the IRS bio-assays and manage the routine entomological surveillance at the 16 sites.

The widespread use of DDT in Zimbabwe presents another set of challenges; USAID regulations require another approved SEA that includes DDT be in place before USG funding can support any DDT-related activity. Since Zimbabwe almost equally uses DDT and pyrethroids for IRS, it can be challenging for the implementing partner to carry out nationwide activities until the lengthy SEA process is complete. The GoZ issued a formal letter saying that early or mid-2014 would be more convenient for the country for the GoZ. Another challenge is the successful procurement (by non-USG stakeholder) of quality-assured DDT;, a single manufacturer in the world and limited demand result in supply issues.

Proposed activities with FY 2014 funding ($1,814,000)

PMI will continue to fill gaps in IRS funding not covered by the Global Fund or the NMCP. PMI will continue support of IRS in 17 districts in the three most high-burden provinces: Manicaland, Mashonaland East and Mashonaland West, and expand to cover the remaining five pyrethroid districts in the country. This will increase PMI's IRS support from 17 districts to 22 districts, and ensure all of the pyrethroid spraying districts will have PMI support. PMI estimates that 660,000 structures will be sprayed, covering 1.5 million people with FY 2014 funds. While the non-pyrethroid districts will not receive direct PMI support for operations, they will receive indirect support via inclusion in national-level IRS activities, such as: higher-level training, national review and planning meetings, and technical assistance with environmental practices and M&E.

Table 8: Provinces and districts receiving PMI support for IRS

Province	District	Target Rooms	Target Population
Manicaland	Chipinge	100,639	135,304
	Mutare	94,967	116,687
	Mutasa	82,710	92,800
	Nyanga	71,974	94,972
	Chimanimani	62,192	76,922
	Buhera	39,651	73,841
	Makoni	46,214	56,949
Total		**498,347**	**647,475**
Mashonaland East	Mudzi	88,088	138,774
	UMP	86,775	115,236
	Murewa	56,811	85,124
	Mutoko	89,337	131,136
Total		**321,011**	**470,270**
Mashonaland West	Kariba	21,314	36,833
	Chegutu	17,228	23,304
	Hurungwe	47,742	137,058
	Kadoma	39,013	54,325
	Zvimba	19,830	25,851
	Makonde	48,442	67,396
Total		**193,569**	**344,767**
Total: 17 districts in 3 provinces		**1,012,927**	**1,462,512**

Note: The above table lists the NMCP indicator as rooms; for the purposes of PMI reporting structures will be used instead.

Specific activities to be supported by PMI with FY 2014 funding include:

1. *Support spray operations:* Support to fill gaps in IRS in all pyrethroid districts covering 50% of the population in the 45 targeted districts: approximately 660,000 structures and 1.5 million people. Support will include training, planning meetings, environmental compliance, and technical assistance to the NCMP. *($1,590,000)*

2. *Entomological surveillance and monitoring:* Zimbabwe plans to maintain 16 entomological monitoring sites throughout the country, with the NIHR serving as a reference laboratory for molecular identification and determination of insecticide resistance mechanisms. PMI will continue to support entomological surveillance in some of the existing sites. The exact number of sentinel sites will be determined once the sentinel site assessment takes place. Entomological surveillance activities will include adult and larval mosquito surveillance to assess the impact of IRS activities in targeted districts, and bioassays to determine IRS longevity on treated surfaces. *($200,000)*

3. *Procure entomological supplies:* PMI will provide insecticide resistance monitoring equipment for entomological activities to the central NIHR lab. *($10,000)*

4. *Technical assistance to PMI IRS activities*: One CDC technical assistance visit to support entomology, including enhanced insecticide resistance monitoring. *($12,000)*

3. Malaria in Pregnancy

Control of malaria in pregnancy (MIP) was adopted as a policy in Zimbabwe in 2004 to be implemented in the moderate to high-burden malaria transmission areas, with 30 districts designated for MIP interventions (see map below of 30 MIP target districts). The policy is a three-pronged approach that recommends intermittent preventive treatment (IPTp) with sulfadoxine-pyrimethamine (SP) as the drug of choice, distribution and promotion of use of LLINs during pregnancy, and early and effective diagnosis and treatment of clinical malaria. The policy specifically recommends three doses of IPTp with the first dose recommended to be administered after quickening, the second dose given between 26-28 weeks, and the third dose between 34-36 weeks of gestational age. The current NMCP policy is restrictive and needs to be updated to be consistent with the newly released WHO guidelines for IPTp which recommend administration of IPTp at every antenatal care (ANC) visit as early as possible in the second trimester, and as long as they are at least four weeks apart and up until the day of delivery. Adoption of the WHO guidelines will simplify the implementation of the IPTp for health workers and likely increase the uptake of IPTp. Each dose of SP is to be administered to the pregnant woman under a health worker observation. Pregnant women on co-trimoxazole prophylaxis should not be administered IPTp.

Figure 7: Map of Zimbabwe showing IPTp recommended districts, 2013

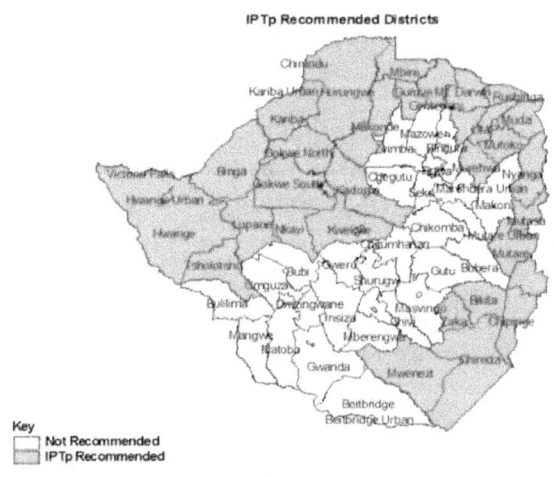

Antenatal attendance in Zimbabwe is very high with 90% of pregnant women visiting ANC at least once during pregnancy, 65% visiting ANC four or more times, and 65% of pregnant women delivering at a health facility (DHS 2010-11). The 2012 MIS showed that 48% of pregnant women attending ANC received SP and 35% received two or more doses of SP. Among women of child-bearing age (15-49 years) 49% slept under an LLIN the night preceding the survey.

Progress during the past 12 months

A total of 567,000 treatments of SP has been procured using FY 2012 funds. During the past twelve months, PMI supported the NMCP to review the training manuals of VHWs and updated the section on MIP. Even though VHWs do not give IPTp in the communities, they do advise pregnant women on MIP. VHWs encourage early antenatal visits, uptake of IPTp, timely presentation at antenatal care, and consistent use of ITNs. PMI has also engaged the NMCP on updating the national policy to reflect the WHO recommendations. With FY 2013 funds, approximate 500,000 treatments will be procured, and PMI staff will work closely with the NMCP and the MOH Reproductive Health Staff to review and revise the national guidelines for implementing IPTp to ensure that the Zimbabwe policy is consistent with the recent WHO revised guidance.

Plans and justification

With FY 2014 funds, PMI will provide support in the MIP implementing districts for the training and supportive supervision of district and health facility level staff on the newly revised MIP implementation guidelines. This training will be part of comprehensive maternal health care delivery training and will aim to improve the uptake of IPTp by improving demand for ANC service. Other MIP topics to be discussed during the training include ITN promotion and malaria case management for pregnant women. Technical assistance will also be provided to improve the forecasting and distribution of SP to the target health facilities to ensure a stable supply. PMI will also procure and distribute approximately 285,000 treatments of SP.

Challenges, opportunities, and threat

The Zimbabwe Informed Push system (ZIPS) of drug and supply distribution has improved the availability of medications in health facilities but there still remain inefficiencies in the system resulting in some health facilities occasionally running short of certain medications, particularly SP. Routine pharmaceutical and supply chain audits have uncovered SP stocked in health facilities outside of the 30 districts targeted by the NMCP for IPTp. The stock imbalances of SP (stockouts of SP targeted districts, and SP availability in non-targeted districts) indicate that more attention is needed to correct the imbalances and health facility staff should be trained on the SP policies. In addition, improvements are needed for the national quantification of SP annually given that the central drug warehouse has had shortages at various times during the year.

Proposed activities with FY 2014 funding ($30,000)

1. *Procurement of SP*: PMI will procure approximately 285,000 treatments of SP for distribution to health facilities located in the target districts for IPTp. Technical assistance will also be provided to improve the quantification and forecasting of SP to ensure a stable supply annually. ($30,000).

2. *Support health worker training and supervision in MIP*: PMI will support the training of health workers in the newly revised implementation guidelines for IPTp, the support will cover the 30 districts designated for MIP interventions to guide pregnant women to follow the recommended IPTp best practices which include completing three doses of sulfadoxine-pyramethamine, use of LLINs during pregnancy and early and effective diagnosis and treatment malaria. The training will also include data recording and reporting. This training and supportive supervision support will benefit health center nurses and ANC nurses in the district hospitals (*see case management training section for funding information*).

4. Case management: Diagnosis

NMCP/PMI Objectives

Since August 2010, the NMCP's policy has been to have parasitological confirmation of all suspected malaria cases by microscopy or RDT before prescribing treatment. Exceptions to this policy are made in the case of malaria epidemics or stockouts of diagnostic tests at the health facility. Rapid diagnostic tests and/or microscopy are typically used for malaria diagnosis at all health facilities, with the exception of primary health facilities where only RDTs are available. Monospecies *P.f.* RDTs are used in 80% of the country with multispecies ones used in the pre-elimination region of Matebeleland South province.

Zimbabwe has 5 central hospitals, 8 provincial hospitals and 68 district hospitals, 4 of which are situated in urban areas; all of these facilities have laboratories.

The Department for Laboratory Service is located under the Directorate of Curative Services of the MOHCW, and is funded primarily by the GoZ. This department is responsible for policy formulation and organizes supervision and refresher training of laboratory personnel. The department's activities are conducted in collaboration with the Tuberculosis Reference Laboratory in Bulawayo, National Virology Laboratory at the University of Zimbabwe medical school, and the National Microbiology Reference Laboratory. Through Global Fund support, about 200 microscopes were purchased under the tuberculosis program. The Ministry supplies laboratory reagents but the quantities are usually not sufficient to meet all needs.

Zimbabwe has three main cadres of facility-based laboratory staff: clinical scientists with a master or doctorate-level degree; general laboratory scientists with a bachelor's degree from the university; and state certified laboratory technicians who receive two years of training post-high school at the polytechnic level. A professional registry, the Medical Laboratory and Clinical Scientist Council, accredits personnel before they can practice. The microscopists currently employed in the health services are paid through the Global Fund Round 8 so at the end of the grant it will be difficult to retain them as there is a hiring freeze in the government sector.

According to the NMCP, parasitological diagnosis of malaria has been fully rolled out to all health facilities and technical assistance visits to a sample of facilities confirmed the availability of malaria microscopy and RDTs. All of the twelve facilities visited consistently have available microscopy, RDTs or both. As a result, and as required by policy, all malaria cases are laboratory confirmed. Health centers have mainly RDTs but a few of the health centers visited also had microscopy capability with trained microscopists who perform both TB and malaria microscopy. In facilities with both RDTs and microscopy, RDTs are mainly used at the outpatient department for testing suspected malaria cases prior to seeing the clinician.

Standard quality control samples for malaria RDTs are lacking globally. However, two of the visited facilities described above have a QC method in the facility in which samples confirmed to be positive by microscopy are used to check RDT performance once to twice a month. This QC method is always performed with a different sample because samples can deteriorate. The QC samples are used no dilution or information on parasite density. This method is unstructured and there are no plans in place for characterizing the samples or for addressing any perceived failure of RDTs.

The microscopy QA/QC system involves the NMRL, and provincial and district hospitals have microscopy supervisors in place who conduct on-site visits. Quarterly integrated trainings for malaria and TB have been conducted in the past for supervisors. However, due to inadequate funding for malaria, most of their supervisory activities are centered on TB.

The health facilities with microscopy capability often conducted internal quality control by making smears from samples collected from patients already diagnosed as positive or negative. A positive and negative smear are stained every week and read. Results are always recorded in the laboratory notebook. Some slide collection by districts supervisors occurred in the past.

Through the Global Fund Round 5 award, ZINQAP, in collaboration with NMCP and NMRL, conducted quarterly on-site supervisors and a proficiency testing program for malaria microscopy as part of a system wide QA program. The funding for this QA program ended with the Global Fund Round 5 award. However, ZINQAP used other funding sources to continue to administer a quarterly proficiency testing program that sends two blinded smears to health facilities. The facilities, treating slides as they would routine samples, stained them and sent reports to ZINQAP. However, due to inadequate funding for the program, follow up testing was not done in instances of low performance. Instead, ZINQAP reported deficiencies to the MOH who are responsible for follow up.

To improve case management, in 2009, national policy was changed to allow VHWs to use ACTs and RDTs. However, limited funding support of health worker and VHW training and procurement of laboratory commodities for diagnosis, including RDTs, has impeded progress in case management. Also, the difficult national economic conditions have resulted in high turnover of health workers leaving inadequate numbers of qualified and trained workers. A review of historical records shows that of 18,000 health workers who were earmarked for malaria training (case management/MIP/RDTs), approximately 10,000 have ever been trained. This figure must also be considered by taking into account high staff attrition.

Despite these challenges, improvements in malaria case management have occurred. More recent reports indicate that more than 8,000 health workers were trained in malaria case management and M&E and 1,325 of the required 6,600 VHWs have trained in RDTs and ACT treatment by the end of 2011. The malaria testing rate improved from 60% in 2009 to 89% in 2011 and recent gaps in RDT needs have been minimal (see Table 9). Additionally, the problem of a lack of a standardized malaria curriculum was recently corrected when a PMI implementing partner facilitated its creation.

Table 9. Rapid Diagnostic Tests Gap Analysis, 2013-2015

	CY 2013	CY2014	CY2015	Totals
Total needs	2,087,315	2,795,830	3,235,450	8,118,595
Commitments	2,087,315	2,795,830	0	4,883,145
Gap	0	0	3,235,450	3,235,450

Progress during the past 12 months

With PMI support, 300 health facility staff have been trained on malaria diagnosis and case management, a proportion of lower-level laboratory staff have been trained on RDT use and slide preparation, and 1,640 VHWs have been trained on community-based case management. This support supplements NMCP's training of 1,412 health workers, which exceeded their target of 1,112. Coverage with RDTs has improved as commitments have met needs. Following a diagnostics technical assistance visit, recommendations for the Zimbabwe malaria diagnostics program including QA/QC were provided. Additionally, PMI supported an assessment of the VHW malaria logistics system.

Challenges, opportunities, and threats

While most clinical and laboratory scientists are quite proficient, laboratory technicians and microscopists would benefit from refresher training on general laboratory procedures, malaria microscopy, and RDT work as well as availability of malaria microscopy and RDT job aids. Although laboratory supervision is inadequate, USG restrictions on work with the GoZ make it difficult for PMI to support MoHCW staff to facilitate supervisory visits. Given the scale up of diagnostic capacity that has occurred, focus needs to be directed on quality assurance in order to maintain and further the gains. There is a possibility of NMCP requesting support for diagnostic training and QA/QC in its concept note for the new Global Fund model. Nationwide the supply chain management of laboratory reagents for malaria slide preparation is inadequate, causing some laboratories to use RDTs even though they have microscopes. Another challenge is the need for an adequate supply of commodities, especially RDTs, for VHWs to ensure that they always test first and do not treat cases clinically. However, an assessment of the VHW malaria logistics system identified problems, such as delays between training and provision of supplies, stockouts, and supply chain challenges, and proposed recommendations.

PMI will continue to support training and will facilitate supervision of 1,200-1,300 health workers in the calendar year 2014 which should help span the gap to cover untrained nurses in the 30 high burden malaria districts and possibly cover refresher training for nurses in specific districts. Using FY 2014 funding, PMI plans to continue to support a similar range of refresher training for health workers but emphasize more on supportive supervision. PMI will also support training of VHWs. Currently the World Bank is providing additional capacity building by supporting a group of partners to revitalize integrated supportive supervision during the next year.

The Global Fund is the other major donor committed to NMCP support. However, the current grant concludes December 2014. The Global Fund plans to support the training of 1,056 health workers during calendar year 2013, and another 1,056 health workers during calendar year 2014. The future plans for Global Fund for health worker training during most of FY 2014 is unknown at this time even though a new grant under the new funding model is anticipated and a gap analysis has already been submitted to the Global Fund. An optimistic estimate of the new funding model start date, should the concept note be successful, is January 2014. At that point PMI/Zimbabwe will have a more complete picture of what Global Fund will support.

Proposed activities with FY 2014 funding ($2,802,000)

1. *Procure RDTs for malaria diagnosis:* PMI will procure approximately 3 million RDTs to complement those procured through the Global Fund. The RDTs will be used at both health facilities and the community level. *($2,630,000)*

2. *Support quality assurance for diagnostics:* PMI will support quality assurance of malaria diagnostics to improve malaria case detection, via a local implementing partner. PMI will also explore the possibility of using the same partner support laboratory supervision. This activity will build upon existing QA systems and help to build capacity. *(110,000)*

3. *Laboratory Supplies:* Support supplementary procurement of laboratory reagents and basic supplies *($50,000)*

4. *Technical assistance visit:* by a CDC laboratory expert to provide technical support to the NMCP on malaria diagnostics, including RDT implementation. *($12,000)*

5. *Support the training of staff at health facilities:* on microscopy slide preparation and RDTs, as appropriate. This activity is co-funded with Global Fund and is part of malaria case management training. *(Costs included in case management training)*

6. *Support the scale up of the training and supervision of village health workers:* on malaria case management and diagnosis using RDTs. This activity will be co-funded with Global Fund. *(Costs included in case management training)*

5. Case management: Pharmaceutical and Commodities Management

NMCP/PMI Objectives

Essential medicines and medical supplies, including malaria commodities, are managed by the Zimbabwe Essential Drugs Action Program, with NatPharm responsible for the procurement, storage, and distribution. This had been a traditional pull system, in which primary health facilities send their orders to the district, which then consolidates orders and places them with the regional NatPharm branch. The economic crisis has further undermined this underfunded system which, along with low product availability, an inconsistent transportation/delivery system, weak reporting, poor communication, low staff morale due to low salaries and brain drain, contributed to the inefficiency of the system and frequent stockouts.

In September 2009, the MoHCW with partners support began a pilot delivery system to improve tuberculosis and malaria drug distribution to primary health facilities and gather logistics data. The ZIPS is essentially a mobile warehouse, which stops quarterly at each primary health facility to assess the stock status, and then based on consumption data, stock on hand and losses/adjustments, tops the facility up to the maximum stock (six months) for all commodities.

The ZIP system distributes malaria, TB, and 26 selected essential medicines and medical supplies to approximately 1,500 service delivery points every quarter. The MoHCW Department of Pharmacy Services, in conjunction with NatPharm, provides leadership to the ZIP system, including leading the annual national quantification process and trimesterly updates. The quantification of malaria commodities is integrated with that of other program commodities such as TB, HIV/AIDS, opportunistic infections, and other essential medicines and medical supplies.

The ZIPS team also re-distributes stocks within the system if a facility has a shortage or soon-to-expire stocks. After a six month pilot, the MOHCW decided to roll out ZIPS nationwide. The ZIP system now reaches 1,534 primary health care facilities on a quarterly basis, and has achieved over 95% distribution coverage and reduced the percentage of stockouts from greater than 30% to less than 5%.[4] In September 2010, the essential medicines and medical supplies were included in the Primary Health Care Package (PHCP), increasing the total number of items managed by ZIPS to approximately 20. The main partners currently supporting implementation of the ZIPS/PHCP system are NatPharm, UNICEF, the USAID/DELIVER PROJECT, and Crown Agents Zimbabwe. Donor funding comes primarily from PMI.

The current plan of the MoHCW is to continue with the ZIPS delivery system and as the economic situation improves, shift back to a traditional NatPharm supported pull system. The MoHCW hopes to pilot a redesigned pull system in 2014. One proposal is to have a hybrid or an assisted pull system, where each facility is still visited quarterly to get the stock counts for all commodities. Once the data are collected, consumption and stock status reports would be turned over to NatPharm, who would then organize and pack the necessary commodities and deliver

---

[4] Overview of malaria commodities supply chain in Zimbabwe, USAID|DELIVER PROJECT, July 2011.

them to the health facilities. USAID implementing partners will provide technical assistance in this effort. The design and pilot activities will to some extent be co-funded by the USG, UNICEF, and Global Fund. Available and additional PMI funds could be allocated to complement funding from other sources.

Progress during the past 12 months

PMI has supported the ZIPS operations, which included other USAID health programs, ensuring that malaria commodities are delivered on a quarterly basis to the approximately 1,500 primary health facilities in Zimbabwe. With FY 2012 funding, PMI and other partners co-funded the distribution of the following quantities of product across the country; 1,085,396 ACT treatments, 1,448,730 RDT tests, and 929,282 SP tablets. PMI supports approximately 33% of the ZIP system. Other partners are UNICEF, DFID, EC, and Global Fund. Although not all health facilities receive malaria commodities, ZIPS also delivers TB and primary health care packages, hence paying quarterly visits to all facilities. The funding supports the fuel and maintenance of the 18 delivery trucks, per diem for the drivers, the automated software as well as the technical assistance and supervision for entire system. The quantification process, including updates every trimester, is led by the Directorate of Pharmacy Services in consultation with the NMCP.

Plans and justification

PMI will continue to support the implementation of ZIPS in order to ensure that malaria commodities, such as ACTs, RDTs, severe malaria medicines, and SP, are available in health facilities. PMI also plans to support a system redesign once a plan is agreed upon by the MoHCW and stakeholders.

Challenges, opportunities, and threats

Rapid diagnostic tests and ACTs were generally available in full supply in 2012 with less than 10% stockout rates at health facilities (Source: NatPharm TOP UP electronic database*)*; however funding gaps continued to exist for SP and quinine tablets. PMI has become the main source of SP and quinine tablet supply in Zimbabwe, coming to the aid of the MoHCW to address shortages in 2013 and 2014. Operational and cash flow challenges (for paying per diems, fuel, maintenance and repairs of trucks) experienced by partners supporting the distribution system resulted in delays in commencing deliveries as well as protracted deliveries. Although malaria logistics data is now widely available, it is often not submitted in a timely fashion, making it difficult to make decisions. There is room to improve data quality by strengthening capacity building, support and supervision activities at provincial and district level. Logistic management information systems data strengthening could also be achieved through data quality workshops at provincial and/or district level.

The actual consumption of RDTs and ACTs at the health facility level exhibits geographical and seasonal variations, resulting in supply and delivery challenges for the ZIPS. In addition, little information is available on the consumption levels for RDTs and ACTs by the new cadre of VHWs who are currently being trained in RDT use and dispensing ACTs at the community level. The VHWs are given an initial supply of 25 RDTs, 12 ACT treatments, and a register, once they complete their training. VHWs are supposed to come to their designated health facility monthly to report their consumption and for resupply so that their ACT and RDT requirements are included in the affiliate health center's requirements during ZIP delivery. However, since the actual consumption of RDTs at the health facility level, and projected consumption of ACTs and RDTs by VHWs is not fully known or predictable, there could be supply and delivery challenges for ZIPS.

Another challenge for the ZIPS is tied to the USG restrictions in Zimbabwe, and PMI's partnership with Global Fund, and DfID, via Crown Agents Zimbabwe. With each ZIPS trip, the district pharmacy technician joins the delivery team and visits the health facilities. Since USG funds cannot support any MOHCW staff, PMI partners, Global Fund and DfID, have been contributing to the per diems of the district staff. If other partners encounter funding issues, it would be difficult to continue ZIPS operations.

Proposed activities with FY 2014 funding ($780,000)

1. *Support approximately 33% of ZIP distribution system*: Support ZIP system operations to provide ACTs, RDTs, severe malaria medicines and SP to approximately 1,500 health facilities nationwide. Funds will complement other ZIP funding from other partners. PMI support will go towards HMIS forms reproduction, ZIPS trainings, and delivery team support. If a system redesign is agreed upon by the MoHCW and stakeholders the support will be adjusted accordingly. *($780,000)*

6. Case management: Treatment

NMCP/PMI Objectives

In 2004, Zimbabwe adopted artemether-lumefantrine (AL) as its first-line treatment for uncomplicated malaria. When Zimbabwe was awarded the Global Fund Round 5 grant in 2007, the country procured AL and trained health workers on the new policy. Current national policy for the treatment of severe malaria is with parenteral quinine plus doxycycline or clindamycin, or intramuscular artemether or artesunate where available. Quinine plus clindamycin is to be used for children below eight years and pregnant women. Artesunate suppositories for pre-referral treatment of severe malaria, especially in children, is recommended. This new policy will be incorporated into training manuals and treatment guidelines by the second and third quarters of 2013.

Historically, malaria case reporting data has included both laboratory-confirmed and unconfirmed cases. Since 2005, the number of cases diagnosed clinically is decreasing whereas parasitological diagnosis is increasing (see figure 8). As of 2010, the NMCP policy recommends parasitological confirmation of all malaria cases. Malaria case management is theoretically free in public health facilities and at the village level; but at council and church health facilities, user fees are charged, although RDTs and ACTs are free.

Figure 8: Trends in malaria case detection

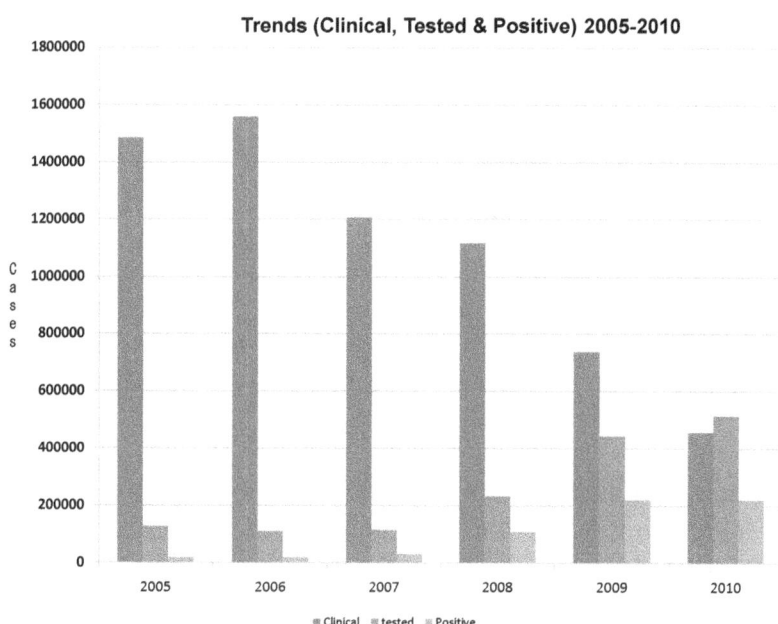

Trends (Clinical, Tested & Positive) 2005-2010

In 2009/10, the NMCP adopted a policy of community case management for malaria and conducted a pilot study to evaluate this program. Trained VHWs follow an algorithm to test all suspected cases with a RDT and treat those with positive results with an ACT. Based on this pilot, the NMCP is scaling up the training of community VHWs to implement community-based treatment on a national scale in malaria endemic districts. The VHWs are selected from their ward by the community. The primary health facility staff is responsible for supervising the VHWs and their data collection. The EHT will be trained to provide VHW supervision. According to the new policy of parasitological confirmation of cases, the NMCP plans to train 6,600 VHWs in malaria case management by 2013

The NMCP, in collaboration with the NIHR, maintains eight therapeutic efficacy monitoring sites, one in each of the rural provinces, where they monitor the efficacy of the first-line malaria treatment. These sites are being supported by the Global Fund. The NMCP acquired a polymerase chain reaction machine from its Global Fund Round 10 grant to support the NIHR to conduct molecular analyses and differentiate re-infection from recrudescence.

Progress during the past 12 months

As stated in the diagnosis section, last year the NMCP trained a total of 1,412 health workers in case management, RDT use, and malaria in pregnancy, exceeding their target of 1,112. PMI supported the training of an additional 300 heath workers. (More detail in diagnosis section.) Comprehensive training of VHWs started late due to the late release of funds from Global Fund but the training is ongoing. In 2010, 90 VHWs were trained; in 2011, 2,893 were trained; and

1,142 VHWs were trained in 2012. Regarding malaria case management, in the past year the NMCP has supported training of 1,851 VHWs countrywide against a target of 1,965 with support from PMI. PMI also procured approximately 500,000 ACTs treatments during the past 12 months.

Therapeutic efficacy studies were conducted at six sites in mid 2013. PMI supported four sites and Global Fund two sites. Final results are pending.

Plans and justification
To enhance access to recommended case management, PMI will procure approximately 1.3 million ACTs. The NMCP is planning to continue to provide training, refresher training, and supportive supervision of health workers. Additionally, the NMCP will accelerate the training of the VHWs as funds become available so that community case management of malaria will be scaled up in the malaria endemic districts, thus improving access to malaria care.

PMI plans to build upon VHW training figures for FY 2013 MOP (estimated 2,800 for FY 2014) and continue to support VHW training in FY 2014 MOP year and also focus on better coordination and advocacy for VHWs, including the use of the standardized curriculum, use of standardized M&E tools and reporting, expansion of a peer supervisor system and promotion of quality performance.

Challenges, opportunities, and threats

Despite the 2009 policy change that allowed the use of ACTs and RDTs by community health workers, the implementation of the community case management of malaria has been slow and uneven. Also, until recently, no standardized malaria curriculum existed. Currently, all eight rural provinces in Zimbabwe have some trained VHWs who test, treat, and track malaria. A four-tier supportive supervision system exists, but is only partially operational. A peer supervisor system has been successfully started in one province.

The MoHCW has estimated that there are 17,000 VHWs total in the country, however that figure refers to a time when VHWs were fully functional; currently, there is not a more reliable estimate nor records detailing which VHWs have been trained. Some VHWs have been trained piecemeal on specific topics by NGOs working in reproductive health, water and sanitation, etc. That being said, Global Fund reports that 11,514 VHWs have received comprehensive training (supported by the Global Fund) from 2009-2012 compared to a target of 11,160 (120 VHWs per district in all districts). Currently, Global Fund states that it actively supports 5,000 VHWs (with $15 stipend, supplies, etc.).

With support from PMI, the NMCP has supported training of 1,851 VHWs, on malaria-specific curricula countrywide; of the target is 1,965 trained VHWs. Approximately 418 additional VHWs were trained with support from other donors: 166 by UMCOR (Mt. Darwin District, Mashonaland Central) and 252 by UNICEF (Mashonaland Central Province). However, during the past year, a few training events could not take place due to logistical challenges with provincial authorities.

In summary, there is a large gap in malaria training for VHWs that PMI alone cannot fill; more work is needed to rationalize the system of support for VHWs. The current malaria Global Fund grant does have some funding to train 879 VHWs in 2014. The majority of the Global Fund training will be concentrated in Matebeleland South Province, the one province in Zimbabwe that is nearing pre-elimination phase. In addition, the rate of attrition of the trained CHWs needs to be monitored, in order to assure that the communities are receiving the necessary services.

Gap Analysis

Table 10. Artemesinin Combination Therapy (ACT) Gap Analysis, 2013-2015

	Calendar Year 2013	Calendar Year 2014	Calendar Year 2015	Totals
Total needs (ACT treatments)				
6 X 1 20/120mg FDC	45,962	257,239	263,794	566,995
6 X 2 20/120mg FDC	68,406	125,950	340,550	534,906
6 X 3 20/120mg FDC	191,568	128,155	294,318	614,041
6 X 4 20/120mg FDC	259,134	361,902	514,974	1,136,010
Commitments				
6 X 1 20/120mg FDC	45,962	257,239	0	303,201
6 X 2 20/120mg FDC	68,406	125,950	0	194,356
6 X 3 20/120mg FDC	191,568	128,155	0	319,723
6 X 4 20/120mg FDC	259,134	361,902	0	621,036
Gap	0	0	1,413,636	

Proposed activities with FY 2014 funding ($2,564,000)

1. *Procure ACTs*: PMI will procure approximately 1.3 million ACT treatments for use in health facilities and by VHWs. *($1,714,000)*

2. Training and supervision for health facility workers: PMI will work with the NMCP to improve malaria case management by supporting the training and supervision of health facility workers. Staff turnover is extremely high in the health system, which affects case management at the facility level. The turnover stem from the current poor working

conditions and low public sector wages. The lack of key skills and capacity, especially at the provincial level, results in a breakdown in service provision and coordination capacity. The training proposed will include ACTs, RDTs, and IPTp, and will be co-funded by Global Fund. ($550,000)

3. *Scale up training and supervision of VHWs in community case management*: PMI will support the training of 650-700 VHW to improve access to the population and the quality of malaria case management at the community level by funding the training and supervision of VHWs on ACTs and RDTs. This activity will be co-funded by Global Fund. *($300,000)*

7. Capacity Building and Health Systems Strengthening

NMCP/PMI Objectives

The NMCP was established to operate at the national and provincial levels and work with the district level to implement malaria programs. The NMCP leads Zimbabwe's malaria control efforts through the formulation of policy strategies, coordination of all partners involved in malaria control in Zimbabwe, and directs the country's current malaria-related Global Fund grants. The NMCP collaborates with several partners including USAID, UNICEF, WHO, CDC, and other international and local institutions to implement the Global Fund projects and PMI. The NMCP has outstanding staff expertise and capacities; however, with increasing funding opportunities, the need for more intensive management and coordination also increases, and additional resources are required for the NMCP to address that need.

Through the Field Epidemiology Training Program, the University of Zimbabwe trains public health personnel in field epidemiology, data analysis, epidemiologic methods, and use of strategic information to make appropriate health decisions. This is a two-year course, which typically benefits central- and provincial- level MoHCW personnel. The University also organizes a short course on leadership and health management for middle-level MoHCW personnel who work at the district level.

In response to the NMCP's various human resource challenges, PMI is invested in training programs at various levels including health facility and VHWs and CHWs. PMI helps fund the supervision of health workers in health facilities involved in the implementation of malaria activities at the health district level. PMI also supports national and provincial meetings, which provide a platform to exchange information and increase communication within the country. PMI will continue to support strengthening and reinforcing the capacity of the logistics management system and overall supply chain management.

Progress during the past 12 months

With FY 2011 and FY 2012 funds, PMI supported the University of Zimbabwe to strengthen the malaria curriculum within the existing FETP program. Funds were made available in February 2013 and are being used to support the new cohort of FETP students that began coursework and training in January 2013. One FETP candidate has been assigned to the NMCP to support their programmatic and monitoring work. In addition, the two PMI Resident Advisors worked closely with the NCMP staff to further enhance the NCMP capacity.

PMI support of additional training programs (e.g. VHWs and health facility workers) was discussed in the Case Management section.

Plans and justification

PMI will continue to support the FETP program in Zimbabwe. PMI and the NMCP will continue to work with the FETP to identify areas to strengthen the malaria portion of the curriculum and provide increased malaria-specific training opportunities and projects for the students.

Challenges, opportunities, threats

The Zimbabwe NMCP has a staff of 12, all of whom are funded through Global Fund grants. At the provincial level, the Provincial Disease Control Officer is responsible for malaria program implementation and monitoring, while at the district level all disease control activities fall on the District Health Director. Due to the economic situation, the staffing and performance at health facilities has been irregular. To fill some of the gaps, the MoHCW has developed an abbreviated training curriculum that is only one year long (instead of three years) to train staff to fill vacant technician and nursing positions. Funding constraints have limited the activities available to the public, and some posts were completely abandoned.

The current USG restrictions prohibit direct funding to the GoZ or any institution affiliated with the GoZ, including the University of Zimbabwe where the FETP students receive their training.

Proposed Activities with FY 2013 Funding: ($100,000)

1. *Support Field Epidemiology Training Program*: Promote malaria-specific field studies and support at least two trainees to enhance field epidemiology skills. The FETP funding is obligated to and managed by the AFENET Cooperative Agreement to provide support for the FETP activities in Zimbabwe. These funds shall provide support for the execution of epidemiologic, outbreak investigation and surveillance evaluation-related activities in Zimbabwe involving the Zimbabwe FELTP. This activity will strengthen mid- to high-level capacity, and develop skilled field supervisors in the malaria field as they learn how to actively seek out, evaluate, and help scale up effective activities against malaria. *($100,000)*

8. Behavior Change Communication (BCC)

NMCP/PMI Objectives

The purpose of Zimbabwe's 2008-2013 National Malaria Communication Strategy is to provide direction and leadership for strengthening malaria BCC interventions in Zimbabwe. The strategy is a key coordination mechanism that defines roles and responsibilities of BCC implementing partners and other stakeholders. The national communication strategy guides districts in developing locally appropriate activities for each of the malaria control interventions and identifies barriers to the desired behaviors as well as problem behavior that compete with the desired behaviors. Target audiences are identified and each control intervention, messages are defined, and a media mix suggested.

During 2013, NMCP plans to extend the National Malaria Communication Strategy through 2015 in line with the current National Malaria Strategic Plan. The NMCP has found that partners willing to work in remote areas on small-scale malaria prevention and treatment activities do not know what to do to assist communities in malaria control. Therefore, to assure that all partners working in Zimbabwe use appropriate communication channels and deliver consistent malaria messages, the NMCP, with support from PMI, is developing malaria BCC implementation guidelines for all BCC implementing partners.

Mobilizing traditional and religious community leaders and civic organizations to support and promote malaria prevention and control is critical for achievement of the NMCP's strategy and PMI objectives. Attached to each primary health facility is one or more Ward Health Team (WHT), comprised of volunteers from the community. The WHTs often include community health workers, school masters, and community leaders who assist with malaria communication for IRS and LLIN distribution campaigns. Community malaria committees are made up of volunteers selected by their communities and trained by the primary health facility staff on key malaria messaging at an interpersonal communication level. With the implementation of community case management of malaria using VHWs, the NMCP is planning to put more emphasis on VHW activities. The VHWs test, treat, and refer for malaria prevention and treatment as warranted and can serve as important conveyors of appropriate health messages and information. To achieve the desired results, the NMCP plans to put emphasis on training activities to strengthening the WHTs and community malaria committees, which often coordinate malaria prevention activities with the VHWs.

In 2011 and 2012, LLIN universal coverage campaigns were the primary focus of the NMCP's BCC efforts and funding. Since Zimbabwe does not have a historical 'net culture,' there is still clearly a lot of work to do to promote consistent net use; however, in 2013 and beyond, the NMCP plans to appeal to partners to expand efforts to increase IPTp uptake and also increase messaging in advance of IRS season, something which was neglected in the 2012 spraying season. While there has been some effort made to encourage early care-seeking for malaria treatment, the NMCP recommends that much more be done in this area, especially in Manicaland Province, which is currently experiencing the highest number of malaria cases in Zimbabwe, and in the remote rural areas along the borders with Mozambique and Zambia. The 2012 MIS and PSI's multi-round surveys from a representative sample of target populations (Tracking Results

Continuously [TRaC]) suggest that community members have confusing definitions for malaria and the symptoms of malaria. For example, while fever is *always* associated with malaria, other common malaria symptoms, such as joint pain and vomiting, are not.

Progress during the past 12 months

During the past year, PMI funding for BCC has been used to improve malaria prevention activities, including the utilization of LLINs and encouraging early care seeking for malaria. Specifically, PMI:

- Supported 5 road-shows in 14 LLIN districts to inform the communities of the importance of LLINs and of how to hang, use, and maintain them properly.

- Supported training of VHWs on communication skills such as how motivate people to discuss malaria issues, both among themselves and with service-providers as well as how to change household practices, mobilize their communities to participate actively in malaria interventions, increase community knowledge about malaria and appropriate steps to take when a family member gets malaria.

- Produced BCC print materials related to correcting misinformation on: causes and pathways of malaria transmission, signs and symptoms of malaria, importance of early diagnosis and appropriate treatment, dangers of self medication and unreliable drugs, and using insecticide treated bed nets. .Supported the analysis of data from the Malaria a TraC household survey conducted in 2008 to assess communities' understanding of malaria transmission, recognition of signs and symptoms, perceptions of cause, treatment-seeking patterns, and preventive measures and practices in order to inform the NMCP's malaria BCC interventions.

The results from the 2008 survey show that the LLIN usage increased from 9% in 2008 to 50% in 2011. Further analyses using propensity score matching comparing between people who have been exposed to BCC activities with people who were not exposed show higher proportion of respondents who slept under an LLIN the night before in the exposed group 71.7% (exposed, N=256, p<0.001) compared to 55% in the groups that were not exposed to the same BCC campaign (N=439, L1=0.112). The print media (leaflets, flyers, posters, and newspapers) and IPC (road shows and drama groups) had the greatest impact on influencing net utilization and compared to mass media. PMI is in the process of evaluating the non-users of nets in line with the same methodologies to build on these results to increase net usage. PMI is currently working with the same implementing partner to analyze the remaining information on the management of fever at the household level.

The funds have also been used to support malaria BCC Working Group within the NMCP responsible for reviewing malaria BCC materials for quality assurance as well as the revisions of the National Malaria Communication Strategy.

Plans and justification

The Global Fund Round Single Stream of Funding (SSF) grant has support for the development and implementation of malaria control communications, via mass-media and community-based activities ($791,977 for 2013 and $837,188 for 2014). PMI support will complement Global Fund activities and, under NMCP guidance focus on inter-personal communication, print materials development, pre- transmission season malaria prevention activities (LLINs, IRS), case management of malaria, and IPTp uptake. Evidence-based messages, focusing on a target audience, are used, and the delivery methods include mass media, interpersonal communication, and print media. While the NMCP's National Communication Strategy does include a monitoring and evaluation component for BCC, support is needed to evaluate specific interventions and actual behavior change.

Challenges, opportunities, and threats

The NMCP coordinates and oversees all malaria-related BCC messaging. The USG restrictions prevent PMI from directly supporting the NMCP staff, which can make BCC rollout and implementation challenging; however, with NMCP in the lead, PMI works through partners to implement BCC activities. In the case of BCC, Global Fund and PMI are working through the same partner which has tremendous coordination advantages.

Proposed activities with FY 2014 funding ($600,000)

> *1. Support malaria BCC:* Support for the development/revision of existing materials, reproduction, dissemination, and evaluation of BCC materials for malaria communications. The FY 2014 funds will be used to expand the deployment of VHW for interpersonal communication in 30 selected districts and support for LLIN distribution (both campaign and routine via ANC and EPI services), improve IPTp uptake (completing three doses of sulfadoxine-pyramethamine, use of LLINs during pregnancy, and early and effective diagnosis and treatment malaria), promote IRS and case management. These funds will also support the malaria BCC Working Group within the NMCP which is responsible for reviewing BCC materials for quality assurance as well as the revisions of the National Malaria Communication Strategy. Overall, PMI-supported BCC activities will primarily promote increasing knowledge and enabling behaviors related to malaria prevention and treatment. *($600,000)*

9. Monitoring and Evaluation

NMCP/PMI Objectives

The NMCP's Monitoring and Evaluation (M&E) Plan was released in 2009 and has been updated and extended to 2015 to align with the National Strategic Plan. The main objective is to reduce the malaria disease burden from 95 per 1,000 population in 2007 to 10 per 1,000 by 2015 and reduce malaria death to near zero by 2015. The M&E plan is based on the Global Fund M&E Toolkit, WHO recommended indicators, and internationally accepted tools and practices related to M&E. The M&E plan defines national malaria indicators, sources and frequency of data collection, measurement procedures, as well as mechanisms to track progress towards targets. Surveillance, M&E and research in malaria have evolved over time with the National Health Information System processing morbidity and mortality data through the recently launched District Health Information System (DHIS). Major M&E activities include nationwide surveys (2012 MIS, 2010/11 DHS), audits, planning and review meetings, rapid assessments, support and supervisory visits to institutions, and routine data collection. Information obtained is used for evidence-based decision making, program management, and accountability.

Surveillance, M&E, and operational research data are collected, reported and recorded from many channels including routine data systems, programmatic monitoring, and national surveys. Additional M&E data are available, including insecticide resistance monitoring and therapeutic efficacy studies. The table below summarizes some of the key monitoring and evaluation data for malaria in Zimbabwe, including national-level surveys, routine and specialized surveillance systems, and other data sources.

Table 9: Key Monitoring & Evaluation Data in Zimbabwe

Data Source	Year								
	2008	2009	2010	2011	2012	2013	2014	2015	2016
Household Surveys		MIMS	DHS (10-11)		MIS	RIA*	MPR* MIMS	MIS/DHS	
Other Surveys		TRaC*		HFS	EUV EA	EUV SEA TRaC		TRaC	
Malaria surveillance and routine system support[3]	HMIS/ GMP database RDNS/ WDSS IDSR	HMIS/ GMP database RDNS/ WDSS IDSR	HMIS/ GMP database RDNS/WDSS IDSR	DHIS/GMP database RDNS/ WDSS IDSR	DHIS/ GMP database RDNS/ WDSS IDSR	HMIS/DHIS2^/ GMP database RDNS/WDSS IDSR	DHIS2/ GMP database RDNS/ WDSS IDSR	DHIS2/ GMP database RDNS/ WDSS IDSR	DHIS2/ GMP database RDNS/ WDSS IDSR
Other Data Sources	Ento monitoring TES	Ento monitoring	Ento monitoring TES	Ento monitoring	Ento monitoring	Ento monitoring TES**	Ento monitoring TES	Ento monitoring TES	Ento monitoring TES

TRaC conducted by PSI; *Supported by WHO and other sources. ^PEPFAR has supported DHIS2 piloting and roll-out for 2013. **WHO supported two additional TES sites
MPR=Malaria Program Review
HFS=Health Facility Survey
HMIS=Health management information system
DHIS2 =District Health Information System
WDSS= Weekly Disease Surveillance System
TES=Therapeutic efficacy study
TRaC= Tracking Results Continuously
GMP=Global Malaria Programme (of WHO)

Routine Data Systems
The main sources of routine malaria data are the National Health Information System (NHIS) and the Weekly Disease Surveillance System (WDSS), a subset of Integrated Disease

Surveillance and Reporting (IDSR). The NHIS has recently implemented a District Health Information System (DHIS) which will form the foundation for the country's HMIS. Monthly reports on malaria cases and deaths from all public health facilities and mission clinics are reported through the DHIS. With regard to malaria, these data include the number of suspected cases, number of suspected cases with parasitologic testing, number of parasitologically-confirmed cases, ACT consumption, and IPTp uptake. DHIS information is currently being reported via paper, from health facilities to district health information officers who enter these data into the DHIS electronic database. Consolidated electronic data are then reported to the ten provincial offices where data are consolidated and reported to the national level. The DHIS was implemented nationally in 2011; training of district and health facility staff is ongoing but has experienced delays due to funding constraints. Other implementation barriers include lack of resources for on-site validation checks, supervisory visits, and staff vacancies at the district and provincial levels. As a result, the system is currently under-performing, with problems related to both the timeliness and completeness of data. Other problems include limited training, supervision, hardware, and difficulty with internet connectivity in some settings. Zimbabwe will be transitioning to DHIS-2, a web-based HMIS reporting system, in 2013. DHIS-2 has been piloted in Manicaland and will be rolled out nationally by the end of 2013 after incorporating feedback from the field experiences.

The WDSS provides weekly data on 12 epidemic-prone diseases, including laboratory-confirmed malaria cases and deaths, from approximately 1,350 health facilities nationwide. The alert epidemic threshold is reached when the number of confirmed weekly cases exceeds the three-year mean of the confirmed weekly cases plus one standard deviation (SD), the action epidemic threshold is reached with the reported weekly cases exceed the three-year mean plus two SDs of reported cases. Threshold calculations issues were reported during a malaria outbreak in early 2013, in that multiple causes were identified including many new facilities that did not have the historical data to calculate the thresholds or facility staff were not properly trained on utilizing the thresholds to recognize and report an increase in cases. Health facilities reporting to WDSS submit data to the districts which then transmit to provincial and central levels. Weekly meetings are held at the national level to review and discuss data quality, potential outbreaks, and action steps. In the case of the 2013 outbreak, the situation was first recognized at the district level. A weekly report is also produced and distributed to the national program areas. During the most recent reporting facilities reporting completeness was approximately 80%.

Programmatic monitoring
Programmatic data on IRS, LLIN distribution, and larviciding are managed by the NMCP using the WHO Global Malaria Database, and are used to monitor and report on the implementation of all malaria control activities. Data are collected from the sub-district level and passed through district and provincial levels to the national level on a weekly, monthly, or quarterly basis, depending on the data being reported. The system was initiated in 2010; full implementation began in late 2011. However, data completeness is an issue with this system as reporting is not always consistent.

National surveys
The most recent DHS was completed in 2010/11 and incorporated a standard malaria module. In April 2009, UNICEF supported a Multiple Indicator Monitoring Survey (MIMS), which is

similar to the MICS and which also included a malaria module. Data from the DHS and MIMS provide pre-PMI baseline estimates (Table 1) for most all coverage indicators used by PMI. PMI supported an MIS in 2012 with anemia and parasitemia biomarkers; in the 51 malaria endemic districts. UNICEF is considering sponsoring another MIMS in 2014 to measure progress towards the Millennium Developmental Goals. The NMCP has begun planning an MIS to be conducted in 2015. The next DHS will likely take place in 2015; however, it is unknown if this will affect UNICEF's plans to conduct the MIMS in 2014.

During 2012, the NMCP, with financial support and technical assistance from the GoZ, Global Fund and PMI and other local institutions, completed an MIS. Key results from the 2012 MIS include the finding of low national parasitemia in children under five years of age: 1% by RDT confirmation and 0.4% by microscopy confirmation, yet high anemia in children under five. Additional findings from the survey include: low ITN utilization, low IPTp uptake, and that radio or TV were not common sources of malaria information.

Multiple end-use verification surveys (a survey to verify availability of malaria commodities in health facilities and warehouses), were conducted in 2012 and 2013. DELIVER has provided quarterly reports summarizing the EUV activities and findings. These quarterly reports provide key observations, recommendations, and next steps and are distributed widely to MoH personnel and in-country partners in Zimbabwe. Additional follow-up surveys are planned to be conducted in FY 2014.

Progress during the past 12 months

To date, 63 of the 285 health workers have been trained in case management; 36 of the 167 targeted staff have been trained in M&E; and 180 of 1,965 community health workers have been trained. In 2013, a national malaria community case management manual and training package was developed and will be used for health care worker trainings, including VHW trainings.

Since 2012, refresher courses on conducting the therapeutic efficacy study have been held at the therapeutic efficacy sites for staff and studies have commenced at four sites (Dindi, Hauna, Nyamhunga, Simatelele), the commodities have also been procured for the four sites.

Plans and justification

With FY 2014 funding, PMI will continue to support malaria surveillance and survey activities. PMI support will continue for M&E trainings at all levels including village and community health workers as well as supervisory and district health facility trainings. In addition, PMI support will be used to facilitate quarterly meetings for district-, provincial- and national-level representatives to meet and discuss surveillance and M&E related issues. PMI will continue to support four therapeutic efficacy study sites yearly. In addition, PMI will support either an MIS or DHS in 2015. The most recent DHS was conducted in 2010 and incorporated a standard malaria module. In April 2009, UNICEF supported a Multiple Indicator Monitoring Survey (MIMS), similar to the MICS in terms of the malaria module that also included a malaria module. Data from the DHS and MIMS provide pre-PMI baseline estimates for most coverage indicators used by PMI. PMI supported an MIS in 2012 with anemia and parasitemia biomarkers.

UNICEF is considering sponsoring another MIMS in 2014 to measure progress towards the Millennium Developmental Goals. However, the next DHS/MIS that is currently being planned for 2015 may affect UNICEF's plans for the MIMS in 2014 as UNICEF has not yet begun to plan their MIMS survey. Given this, it is possible to harmonize the surveys but further discussion is necessary with all of the stakeholders; however, due to the planning requirements of the MOP funds it is necessary to ensure a national survey collecting PMI appropriate indicators and biomarkers is scheduled for 2015. The PMI team will work closely with the survey partners and stakeholders to determine the optimal strategy for collecting the necessary biomarkers.

Challenges, opportunities, and threats

The political situation in Zimbabwe continues to present significant challenges for PMI. Moreover, the recent malaria epidemic in the Manicaland and Mashonaland Central Provinces highlight the precarious nature of the gains made in malaria control. Continual training on M&E and health information systems will improve the capacity for recognizing and responding to epidemics. In addition, the current USG restrictions prohibit giving any funding to the GoZ or any institution affiliated with the GoZ, make it challenging to implement NIHR related therapeutic efficacy sites activities in Zimbabwe, this has led to many delays in the implementation of activities and can possibly impact the sample size for the 2013 therapeutic efficacy collection and potentially affect the quality of the data.

Proposed activities with FY 2014 funding ($1,362,000)

1. *End-use verification survey:* Conduct quarterly surveys to verify availability of malaria drugs and RDTs in health facilities and warehouses. *($100,000)*

2. *Therapeutic efficacy studies:* Continue support of ACT therapeutic efficacy studies of artemether-lumefantrine (AL) in four of the eight designated sentinel sites, in conjunction with NIHR. *($200,000)*

3. *National M&E support:* Support the NMCP to train staff at the regional, district, and health facility levels in routine data collection systems (DHIS-2 and WDSS). The training will include improving data collection, analysis, and reporting. Trainings will support strengthening the quality of malaria data (completeness, accuracy, timeliness, and consistency) at the community, health facility, district, and regional levels. PMI will provide assistance to ensure that the malaria component of the DHIS-2 is implemented consistently across all provinces. IDSR/WDSS training will also be supported to improve capacity to analyze and monitor the malaria trends, and improve preparedness for epidemic response. *($300,000)*

4. *Malaria Indicator Survey or Demographic Health Survey:* Support either an MIS or DHS scheduled for 2015. In Zimbabwe, Global Fund is one of a few partners providing funding for the proposed DHS, however, funding gaps were identified and the amount that PMI is proposing will cover the identified gap. If other partners contribute to the cost of the DHS or MIS then any of the unneeded PMI funding will be reprogrammed toward other PMI activities. *($750,000)*

5. *Technical assistance:* CDC TDY to support PMI Zimbabwe M&E activities. *($12,000)*

10. Staffing and Administration

Two health professionals serve as Resident Advisors to oversee PMI in Zimbabwe, one representing CDC and one representing USAID. In addition, one FSN supports the PMI team. All PMI staff members are part of a single inter-agency team led by the USAID Mission Director in country. The PMI team shares responsibility for development and implementation of PMI strategies and work plans, coordination with national authorities, managing collaborating agencies and supervising day-to-day activities. Candidates for resident advisor positions (whether initial hires or replacements) will be evaluated and/or interviewed jointly by USAID and CDC, and both agencies will be involved in hiring decisions, with the final decision made by the individual hiring agency.

The two PMI professional staff will work together to oversee all technical and administrative aspects of PMI, including finalizing details of the project design, implementing malaria prevention and treatment activities, monitoring and evaluation of outcomes and impact, and reporting of results. Both staff members report to the USAID Mission Director. The CDC staff person is supervised by CDC both technically and administratively. All technical activities are undertaken in close coordination with the MoHCW/NMCP and other national and international partners, including the WHO, UNICEF, the Global Fund, World Bank, and the private sector.

Locally hired staff to support PMI activities either in Ministries or in USAID will be approved by the USAID Mission Director. Because of the need to adhere to specific country policies and USAID accounting regulations, any transfer of PMI funds directly to Ministries or other host government institutions will need to be approved by the USAID Mission Director.

Proposed Activities with FY2014 Funding ($1,500,000)

1. *In country PMI staff salaries, benefits, travel and other PMI administrative costs*: Support for two PMI (CDC and USAID) Resident Advisors and FSN staff members to oversee activities supported by PMI in Zimbabwe. Additionally, these funds will support pooled USAID Zimbabwe Mission staff and mission-wide assistance from which PMI benefits. *($1,500,000)*

Table 1: FY 2014 Funding by Mechanism

Partner	Geographical Area	Activity	Budget ($)	%
DELIVER	Nationwide	Procure and distribute LLINs	$2,000,000	52%
	Nationwide	Procure SP	$30,000	
	Nationwide	Procure RDTs for case management of malaria	$2,630,000	
	Nationwide	Procure diagnostic supplies	$50,000	
	Nationwide	Support for ZIPS distribution system for ACTs and RDTs	$780,000	
	Nationwide	Procure ACTs and severe malaria drugs	$1,714,000	
	Nationwide	End use verification	$100,000	
PSI	Nationwide	Support LLIN distribution	$450,000	15%
	Nationwide	Supportive supervision and training on malaria case management for health facility workers	$550,000	
	Nationwide	Support malaria BCC	$600,000	
	4 sites	Therapeutic efficacy studies	$200,000	
	Nationwide	Support M&E activities, including IDSR/DHIS2, at provincial, district and primary health facility levels	$300,000	
USAID	Nationwide	Provide technical assistance to LLIN activities	$0	6%
	Nationwide	Technical assistance for IEC/BCC	$0	
	Nationwide	In country staffing and administration costs	$900,000	
IRS IQC 2 Task Order 4	22 of 45 IRS targeted districts	Support spray operators training and other IRS implementation activities	$1,590,000	13%
	a portion of the 16 surveillance sites plus Harare	Conduct entomological surveillance and monitoring	$200,000	
CDC/IAA	Nationwide	Entomologic supplies	$10,000	5%
	Nationwide	Technical assistance to IRS activities	$12,000	
	Nationwide	Technical assistance for diagnostics	$12,000	
	Nationwide	FETP	$100,000	
	Nationwide	Technical assistance trip to support M&E	$12,000	

	Nationwide	In country staffing and administration costs	$600,000	
TBD	Nationwide	Strengthen malaria diagnostic capacity	$110,000	6%
	Nationwide	MIS/DHS	$750,000	
MCHIP	Nationwide	Training and supervision of VHWs by health facility workers and EHTs	$300,000	2%
Total			**$14,000,000**	**100%**

Table 2: FY 2014 Planned Obligations for Zimbabwe

Proposed Activity	Mechanism	Total Budget	Commodities	Geographic Area	Description of Activity
ITNS					
Procure and distribute LLINs	DELIVER	$2,000,000	$2,000,000	Nationwide	Purchase approximately 525,000 LLINs for distribution through ANC and child health clinics in high burden malaria districts.
Support LLIN distribution	PSI	$450,000	$0	Nationwide	Strengthen routine LLIN distribution systems and support the supply chain for a continuous availability of LLINs.
Provide technical assistance to LLIN activities	USAID	$0	$0	Nationwide	One USAID TDY to provide support for LLIN distribution (costs covered in core USAID budget).
Subtotal: ITNs		*$2,450,000*	*$2,000,000*		
IRS					
Support spray operators training and other IRS implementation activities	IRS IQC 2 Task Order 4	$1,590,000	$300,000	22 of 45 IRS targeted districts	Support IRS implementation in all pyrethroid districts, including the procurement of equipment and material, training support and other logistics required for spray operations.
Conduct entomological surveillance and monitoring	IRS IQC2 Task Order 4	$200,000	$0	a portion of the 16 surveillance sites plus Harare	Provide support to the NMCP and NIHR for comprehensive entomological surveillance.
Entomologic supplies	CDC/IAA	$10,000	$10,000	Nationwide	Procure entomological supplies necessary for entomological surveillance.
Technical assistance to IRS activities	CDC/IAA	$12,000	$0	Nationwide	One CDC TDY to provide support for entomological activities.
Subtotal: IRS		*$1,812,000*	*$310,000*		

IPTp					
Procure SP	DELIVER	$30,000	$30,000	Nationwide	Purchase approximately 285,000 treatments of SP for IPTp.
Subtotal: IPTp		$30,000	$30,000		
Case Management: Diagnostics					
Procure RDTs for case management of malaria	DELIVER	$2,630,000	$2,630,000	Nationwide	Purchase approximately 3 million RDTs for use at primary health facilities and by VHWs.
Strengthen malaria diagnostic capacity	TBD	$110,000	$0	Nationwide	Provide technical support for RDTs and microscopy at the district and primary health facility level
Procure diagnostic supplies	DELIVER	$50,000	$50,000	Nationwide	Purchase lab supplies and reagents to support microscopy diagnosis of malaria
Technical assistance for diagnostics	CDC/IAA	$12,000	$0	Nationwide	One CDC TDY to provide support for RDT and microscopy activities.
Subtotal		$2,802,000	$2,680,000		
Pharmaceutical Management					
Support for ZIPS distribution system for ACTs and RDTs	DELIVER	$780,000	$0	Nationwide	Support ZIPS, including operational costs, technical assistance, trainings, quantification support and logistics.
Subtotal		$780,000	$0		
Case Management: Treatment					
Procure ACTs and severe malaria drugs	DELIVER	$1,714,000	$1,714,000	Nationwide	Procure approximately 1.3 million ACT treatments for use at health facilities and with VHW.
Supportive supervision and training on malaria case management for health facility workers	PSI	$550,000	$0	Nationwide	Support training and supervision on malaria case management for primary health facility staff on ACTs, RDTs and MIP.

Activity	Partner			Location	Description
Training and supervision of VHWs by health facility workers and EHTs	MCHIP	$300,000	$0	Nationwide	Support training and supervision on malaria case management for VHW at the community level on ACTs and RDTs.
Subtotal		$2,564,000			
Subtotal: Case Management		$6,146,000	$1,714,000		
Capacity Building					
FETP	CDC/IAA (AFINET)	$100,000	$0	Nationwide	Support malaria-specific field studies and at least two student trainees to enhance field epidemiology skills.
Subtotal: Capacity Building		$100,000	$0		
BCC					
Support malaria BCC	PSI	$600,000	$0	Nationwide	Support malaria BCC for LLINs, MIP and case management, particularly for the VHW. Includes revision of existing materials, reproduction, dissemination and evaluation.
Technical assistance for IEC/BCC	USAID	$0	$0	Nationwide	One USAID TDY to provide support for updating/revising the BCC/IEC strategy.
Subtotal: IEC/BCC		$600,000	$0		
M&E					
End use verification	DELIVER	$100,000	$0	Nationwide	Quarterly surveys to assess availability of malaria commodities in health facilities and warehouses.
Therapeutic efficacy studies	PSI	$200,000	$0	4 sites	Support therapeutic efficacy studies in 4 of the 8 sites. The other 4 sites will be supported with FY 2013 funds.

Activity	Partner			Location	Notes
Support M&E activities, including IDSR/DHIS2, at provincial, district and primary health facility levels	PSI	$300,000	$0	Nationwide	Support quarterly district health team meetings, provincial M&E review meetings, training support and supervision from the provincial level. Funds will also continue to support the IDSR/DHIS2.
MIS/DHS	TBD	$750,000	$0	Nationwide	Support the next large national survey with malaria indicators.
Technical assistance trip to support M&E	CDC/IAA	$12,000	$0	Nationwide	One CDC TDY to support on-going M&E activities in country.
Subtotal: M&E		$1,362,000	$0		
Staffing & Administration					
In country staffing and administration costs	USAID	$900,000	$0	Nationwide	Support for USAID staffing and administration costs
In country staffing and administration costs	CDC	$600,000	$0	Nationwide	Support for CDC staffing and administration costs
Subtotal: Staffing and Administration		$1,500,000	$0		
GRAND TOTAL		**$14,000,000**	**$6,734,000**		